DIRECTED CARE

DIRECTED CARE

Showcasing the Expertise of Professional Nurses in Ambulatory Primary Care

Sharon A. Jamieson, ARNP, MSN, MN

Family Nurse Practitioner

An
APPLE WORKS
Publication

Published by:

Apple Works
PO Box 1122
Puyallup, WA 98371

ISBN: 978-0-9883407-0-1
Library of Congress Control Number: 2012950112

Editor: Draftcrafters
Proofreader: Phil Loyd
Interior and Book Cover Design: Wordzworth Limited

Printed in the United States of America

Dedicated to the professional nurses who uphold the value of the art of nursing and visualize their unique contribution in the delivery of health care services as independent clinical team members rather than competitors to physician endeavors.

Table of Contents

Preface   xi

Acknowledgement   xiii

CHAPTER ONE   U.S. HEALTH CARE SYSTEM LACKS COST-EFFECTIVENESS   1

Contributing Factors to Cost-Ineffectiveness   1

Perspectives of Health Care Consumers   3

Past Approaches to Improve Cost-Effectiveness   3

Engaging Professional Nurse Expertise   4

CHAPTER TWO   MAJOR INFLUENCES ON HEALTH CARE CONSUMER UTILIZATION PATTERNS   9

System Complexity with Administrative Overlay of Clinical Activities   9

Health Care System Organization – Not a Simple View   10

Impact of Information Technology   12

Organization Expense Management Issues   13

Illness Care in the Limelight – A Target for Change   14

Prevalence of Chronic Disease   15

Measures Aimed at Disease Management   16

Change Focus to Preventive Care   17

The Dominant Role of Third Party Payers in Transactions for Health Care Services   19

Health Insurance as a Payer for Health Care Services   19

Connection Lost to Cost and Responsibility   20

CHAPTER THREE   A DISCUSSION ON DIRECTED CARE – SETTING THE STAGE FOR BETTER HEALTH CARE CONSUMER UTILIZATION PATTERNS   27

The Rationale   29

Managing Utilization of Health Care Resources   29

The Role of Professional Nurses   30

Linking to a Patient-Centered Medical Home 33

Moving Preventive Care to the Forefront as an Offensive Strategy 33

Increasing Access to Communication with Health Care Professionals 37

Building the Foundation for DIRECTED CARE 39

The Design Elements 42

Goal 1. Guide Health Care Consumers to Optimal Wellness. 44

Conduct annual Wellness Checks 44

Identify biological, environmental, and behavioral health risks 47

Offer readily available professional nursing consultation 50

Counsel/Coach behavioral change and self-management skill development 55

Goal 2. Provide Order to the Flow of Information in a Complex, Multidimensional Health Care System. 59

Inject planned visits for preventive and chronic care 59

Create an organized, comprehensive Summary Health Care Record 60

Map out an integrated Health Monitoring Plan 67

Goal 3. Analyze Individual Health Care Consumer Utilization Patterns 71

Goal 4. Develop Accountable Units of Service for Independent Professional Nursing Activities in Ambulatory Primary Care 72

CHAPTER FOUR DIRECTED CARE — PUTTING THE PROCESS INTO ACTION 83

CHAPTER FIVE PLANNING PROFESSIONAL NURSE TIME ALLOCATION FOR DIRECTED CARE ACTIVITIES 93

CHAPTER SIX CLOSING REMARKS 101

Bibliography 105

Appendix A Joint Principles of the Patient-Centered Medical Home 115

Appendix B ANA Summary of Standards for Professional Nursing Practice 119

Appendix C Disease Prevention 123

Appendix D Prevention of Injury 127

Appendix E Optimal Mental Health 131

Appendix F   Adult Wellness Checklist   133

Appendix G   Requirements Brief for Medicare Annual Wellness Visits   137

Appendix H   Safeguarding Your Home   141

Appendix I   Situational Leadership Actions to Influence Behavior   145

Appendix J   Chronic Disease Electronic Management System Overview   147

Appendix K   Look-up Table Example for Summary Health Care Record   149

Appendix L   Entry Categories for Summary Health Care Record   153

Appendix M   Medical Plan of Care (Example)   155

Appendix N   Matching Workload to Available Professional Nurse Time   157

Health is the state about which medicine has nothing to say.

—W. H. AUDEN

Preface

This book is a follow-up to the Institute of Medicine (IOM) report, *The Future of Nursing: Leading Change, Advancing Health*, which presents nursing in the position of leadership for a reformed and better integrated, consumer-centered health care system. The report recommends a transformation in the utilization of professional nurses. The Patient-Centered Medical Home is coming to the forefront as a model to manage consumer health care. Its tenets provide more openings to alternative courses in the utilization of professional nurses. DIRECTED CARE will provide complementary activities focused on the whole person as a health-care consumer.

The dominant force in health care delivery should be clinical encounters and communication between providers and consumers. How important is this interaction? Where would health care delivery be without the clinical side? Professional nurses can help shape the daily operational aspect of the health care delivery system. They can use their current and traditional strengths to direct health care consumers to utilize health care services in a more beneficial manner by building consumers' abilities and confidence in determining how and when they seek services. A more effective and efficient health care delivery benefits all. There is an opportunity for professional nurses to establish an independent role with cost-effective service value. Administrators need to value the contribution of professional nurses in the delivery of health care services at the clinical level and provide them with all necessary resources to accomplish their established responsibilities in a timely manner.

The discussion of DIRECTED CARE is a synthesis of related published professional information (books, journals, and Internet sources) and the author's educational background and professional experience. It is not intended to provide precise answers but rather to stimulate thought on innovative possibilities for using professional nurses in clinical practice settings. It is intended that this process occur at the primary care level with health care consumers involved in the decision-making process.

The term *health care consumer* is used throughout the discussion of DIRECTED CARE in lieu of *patient* or *client*. This was done to place them in the light of recipients of services within the health care delivery system and thus entitled to full participation in decision making.

A more in-depth discussion of each component of DIRECTED CARE could have been written. However, it is felt by the author that professionals want the latitude to develop and expand a concept and then adapt it to their given settings. This discussion includes examples of how information could be organized but does not present a complete plan ready for implementation. An important component of DIRECTED CARE, though, is the development of a Summary Health Care Record for each health care consumer to allow health data to be consolidated and organized in a comprehensive format for rapid review of all aspects of a given individual's health status. The Health Monitoring Plan is also introduced as a means to integrate projected preventive and chronic care needs of a health care consumer for the time span of a year.

Computer technology should play an important role in the organization of health data and be seen as a tool for managing data, not as the master of the user. Health data should be readily available, easily obtained, and in a uniform format so that all clinical users can easily read and interpret the data. Health care providers need to be on the design side of information technology applications to develop an efficient user-friendly data entry system that minimizes providers' time for performing that task. Daily users of the information can provide invaluable input for the desired program output.

No assumptions were made about the reader's understanding of health care delivery in a primary care setting. Some of the discussion may seem too basic for some readers, but the intent is to be clear throughout each component of the DIRECTED CARE concept since reader background is varied. The author is laying the ground work for further development and implementation at the practice level.

A great opportunity abounds for professional nurses to step up and participate in the transformation of how they are utilized in the delivery of health consumer-centered care, particularly in the primary care setting. Home health care accepted a similar challenge in the past and is now established as a prominent nursing service.

Acknowledgement

I want to express my sincere gratitude to Pat Andrews for her editing expertise and relentless pursuit of a quality manuscript to outline and communicate the multiple aspects of the "Directed Care" concept. She was also a great coach with her guidance and encouragement throughout the book production process.

Sharon A. Jamieson

Chapter One

U.S. Health Care System Lacks Cost-Effectiveness

It is hard to dispute that the American health care system is in a state of disorder with high cost and sub-par health improvement for those seeking care. The current per capita health care expenditure in the United States is greater by 30 percent than that of any other country in a 2012 study of 12 industrial nations.[1] A 2010 Commonwealth Fund study ranked the United States last in long, healthy, and productive lives as well as in the overall ranking compared to Australia, Canada, Germany, Netherlands, New Zealand, and the United Kingdom.[2] All Americans need to look at why the delivery of their health care services rates this level of effectiveness and efficiency and to develop an awareness of how they can make a difference.

Contributing Factors to Cost-Ineffectiveness

1. A complex, disorganized health care system

The American health care system is a web of organizations which lack standardization in the central system operational processes. Care is provided at multiple levels by varied organizations with an array of providers. Disorganization is accentuated by limited or no communication between health care providers in a multiple-level system. The third party payer agreements often dictate which health care service providers are utilized without consideration to the coordination of care. This fragmented and disorganized delivery system is a major contributor to rising costs and disappearing quality.[3] The American health care system needs to be more efficient in the way it delivers health care and communicates to consumers of the health care services.

2. An illness-focused system

The current health care system emphasizes treatment of illness with specialist care rather than disease prevention, despite the fact that money spent on evidence-based prevention is money well spent from a cost-effective perspective.[4] The Centers for Disease Control and Prevention reports 75 percent of all health care costs stem directly from preventable chronic disease conditions.[5] "Only 1 percent of the $1.9 trillion dollars spent on health care in the United States is devoted to protecting health and preventing illness and injury."[6] As an illness-focused health care system, the American health care delivery approach needs system-wide re-engineering to be more effective in improving the health of its population and in containing costs. Health care consumers need to be focused on how to prevent illness and injury or how to minimize their effects.

3. Health care consumer loss of connection to cost with third party payment for services

Health care consumers often do not know what services actually cost or what fees have been charged. This creates a loss of connection to price and value. Health care service fees often vary for the same service depending on agreements between provider organizations and third party payers. A health care consumer will be charged full fees if the provider is out of plan or if the consumer has no health insurance. Therefore, the cost is not consistent and floats to the third party administrator's agreement or the individual consumer's payment circumstances. All health care consumers need to be connected to the cost of health care services and be actively involved in purchase decisions.

Perspectives of Health Care Consumers

Where do health care consumers seeking care for themselves or, as parents/guardian of others, fit into this disorder? Health care consumers must deal with resource allocation problems surrounding what, when, and with whom health care services are provided. They are confronted with the web of disconnected health care delivery organizations for services at an inconsistent and probably unknown cost. Accessibility of services, often dictated by method of payment and/or age group, is inconsistent among the health care organizations. Health care consumer utilization patterns for services often reflect a reactive approach to dealing with the "now" or present demand issue – a new symptom, an accident, a chronic care problem. They will be most likely to go to a readily available, convenient resource unless known limitations.

Past Approaches to Improve Cost-Effectiveness

Efforts have been made within the health care system to address the issues of effective and efficient utilization. Case management was developed in the 1970s to help channel health care consumers to the timely utilization of specific services. Its primary focus was individuals who had experienced a catastrophic event which naturally exhibited a high utilization pattern. The second approach was disease management that targeted coordinating elements of managing a chronic condition. Even though a health care consumer receives a benefit from both approaches, the driver for case management was often cost containment for the third party payer.

Over a decade ago, the Institute of Medicine (IOM) published a report, *Crossing the Quality Chasm: A New Health Care System for the 21st Century*, that found the American health care system was in need of an essential organizational change. Serious quality concerns identified within the U.S. health care system were fragmented care, patient safety issues, lack of care coordination, and poor reimbursement for primary care providers.[7] To further emphasize today's need for re-engineering or redesigning the health care system, Champus and Greenspun state: "Inefficient and ineffective health care can take its toll in human lives while devouring our personal and national wealth and resources."[8]

A new generation of care coordination has started to gain momentum – the Patient-Centered Medical Home (PCMH). It evolved from a model first used in 1967 by pediatricians for children with special needs to address the concerns over continuity of care. A Patient-Centered Medical Home is a clinic where care is ongoing and incorporates health promotion and disease prevention. This type of clinic includes a whole person orientation to care with shared health care management. This approach has greater potential for active participation of health care consumers in the delivery of health care services. The Joint Principles of the Patient-Centered Medical Home have a strong resemblance to the findings for redesign outlined by the 2001 IOM report.[9] These Joint Principles are endorsed by several provider organizations and are available in Appendix A for review. Even though the model was first promoted as a physician-led coordinated primary care concept, advanced nurse practitioners have made a surge to play a prominent role. Both the advanced nurse practitioner and registered nurse can play key professional leadership roles in this model of care by connecting the links for effective and efficient utilization of health care services for health care consumers through independent care management activities.

Engaging Professional Nurse Expertise

How can a health care consumer better match appropriate utilization of health care services to need? Professional nurses are the optimal health care provider to intervene and provide direction to health care consumers, assisting with navigating the system and mapping out individual health plans of care aimed toward "getting healthy and staying healthy," as expressed in the National Prevention and Wellness Month motto.[10] Guiding health care consumers through the current maze created by a complex system of multiple levels of providers and lack of universal organizational structure will be an important step toward more efficient use of health care services.

The intent of presenting this vision of the DIRECTED CARE concept is to address the problems of effective and efficient health care delivery from the health care consumers' perspective rather than that of an organization. The theory for this approach is that the way health care consumers utilize the services will reflect the performance of the health care system. Traditional and current professional nurse expertise can provide invaluable input to re-engineer a system for an organized, proactive approach to health care delivery. DIRECTED CARE proposes a structure to channel health care consumer demand for services toward improved health and cost containment by providing a wellness focus, organization of the health care consumer's data base, a health monitoring plan for projected wellness and illness care needs, and health consultation and counseling as needed.

The term *health care consumer* is used throughout the discussion of DIRECTED CARE. Health care consumers create the demand side for health care services while the providers form the supply side. The terms *patient* or *client* can signify that their role is merely that of recipients of services in a more passive state. Children are technically speaking recipients of services or consumers. However, for the purpose of the discussion of DIRECTED CARE, health care consumer will refer to the individual responsible for daily care management, either for oneself or as parent or guardian.

DIRECTED CARE will reinforce an active participant role for health care consumers to become empowered to accept the reins for health management. However, not everyone is at the same level of confidence and ability for making daily choices toward "getting healthy and staying healthy." DIRECTED CARE is geared to assist the maturation process in decision making with professional nurse leadership.

In summary, the overall premise for the large per capita investment in health care expenditure occurring without a corresponding health improvement is the manner in which health care consumers utilize the American health care system. DIRECTED CARE is posed to make a difference in health care consumers' utilization patterns and reconnect them to the system as a consumers of essential services, which ultimately will result in cost containment and improved health.

Notes

1. Commonwealth Fund. "U.S. Spends Far More for Health Care than 12 Industrialized Nations, but Quality Varies" (May 3, 2012), 1, *http://www.commonwealthfund.org/News/News-Release/2012/May/US-Spends-Far-More-for-Health-Care-Than-12-Industrialized-Nations-but-Quality-Varies.aspx* (accessed July 3, 2012).

2. Karen Davies, Cathy Sohoen, and Kristof Sromikis. "Mirror, Mirror on the Wall. How the Performance of the U.S. Health Care System Compares Internationally,. 2010 Update," Commonwealth Fund, no. 1400 (June 2010), v, *http://www.commonwealth.org/-/media/Files/Publications/Fund%20Report/2010/Jun/1400_Davis_Mirror_Mirror_on_the_wall_2010.pdf* (accessed July 3, 2012).

3. Thomas H. Lee and Robert A. Berenson. "The Organization of Health Care Delivery: A Roadmap for Accelerated Improvement." Chap. 2 in *The Health Care Delivery System: A Blueprint for Reform.* Center for American Progress and the Institute on Medicine as a Profession (2008), 33, *http://www.americanprogress.org/issues/healthcare/report/2008/10/the-health-care-delivery-system-a-blueprint-for-reform/* (accessed June 20, 2012).

4. National Business Group on Health. *Payment Systems, Government Policies and Market Incentives Should Refocus Efforts on Disease Prevention.* (Washington, DC, 2010), 1, *http://www.businessgrouphealth.org/pdfs/preventioncarepositionstatement.pdf* (accessed June 20, 2012).

5. Centers for Disease Control and Prevention (CDC). "Chronic Diseases: The Power to Prevent; The Call to Control" National Center for Chronic Disease Prevention and Health Promotion (2009), 2, *http://www.cdc.gov/chronicdisease/resources/publications/AAG/pdf/chronic.pdf* (accessed July 3, 2012).

6. National Business Group on Health. *Payment Systems, Government Policies and Market Incentives Should Refocus Efforts on Disease Prevention.* (Washington, DC, 2010), 2, *http://www.businessgrouphealth.org/pdfs/preventioncarepositionstatement.pdf* (accessed June 20, 2012).

7. Institute of Medicine. *Crossing the Quality Chasm: A New Health System for the 21st Century* (Washington, DC: National Academy Press, 2001), 2.

8. Jim Champy and Harry Greenspun. *Reengineering Health Care: A Manifesto for Radically Rethinking Health Care Delivery* (Upper Saddle River, NJ: Pearson Education, 2010), 2.

9.   Patient-Centered Primary Care Collaborative *Joint Principles of Patient-Centered Medical Home*, (March 2007), 1-3, *http://www.pcpcc.net/ joint-principles* (accessed February 10, 2011).

10. Kathleen Sebelius. "This June, Get Healthy, Stay Healthy," *Healthcare Blog.* Department of Health and Human Services (June 06, 2011), 1, *http://www.healthcare.gov/blog/2011/06/prevention062011a* (accessed August 21, 2011).

Chapter Two

Major Influences on Health Care Consumer Utilization Patterns

With the stated position that health care consumers' utilization of services has a correlation to overall cost-effectiveness, a more in-depth discussion of the factors contributing to their utilization is warranted, since these factors impact the way a health care consumer enters and flows through the system, as well as the resulting costs. Decision making to obtain the right service, at the right time, and from the right provider is a difficult process in the current health care system.

System Complexity with Administrative Overlay of Clinical Activities

Major contributions to this problem are the complexity of the system and the health care consumer's lack of knowledge of how the system operates. In addition, constraints may be placed by whatever health insurance plan administers payment for contracted services. Health care consumers can be left with a feeling of being out of control and pushed and pulled through the system rather than having a clear destination point. The administrative system can often appear complex and impersonal, leaving the health care consumer feeling unimportant and disassociated as a key player in the process of health care delivery.

Health Care System Organization – Not a Simple View

Health care systems can be closed or open. They may have many similar characteristics, but there are several different variations of system organization within both classifications. Closed systems have all services under the umbrella of a single organization such as Group Health or the Military Health System. Open systems have providers operating in separate delivery systems. Consequently, the way the health care consumer interacts with these systems varies from system to system and is affected by the population served and the manner in which the payment for services is administered. Communications between providers and for the coordination of services essential for continuity becomes more of a challenge in open systems.

The health care system uses multiple levels of providers – primary with general or family physicians; secondary with specialists such as internal medicine or orthopedics; and tertiary with sub-specialists such as cardiologists or endocrinologist. An individual health care consumer may need to interact with various departments. Just to obtain an evaluation and/or to initiate treatment, it may be necessary to be shuttled between laboratory, diagnostic imaging, pharmacy and maybe physical or occupational therapy. Services may be under one roof, like a Wal-Mart, or may be in multiple buildings connected by corridors, or may be in entirely separate buildings, each at a different location. The health care consumer encounters a variety of personnel and check-in procedures in addition to the variance in physical layout.

The illustration in Table 2.1 captures the complexity of the health care system and the need for re-engineering.

Table 2.1. Complexity of U. S. Health Care Delivery System

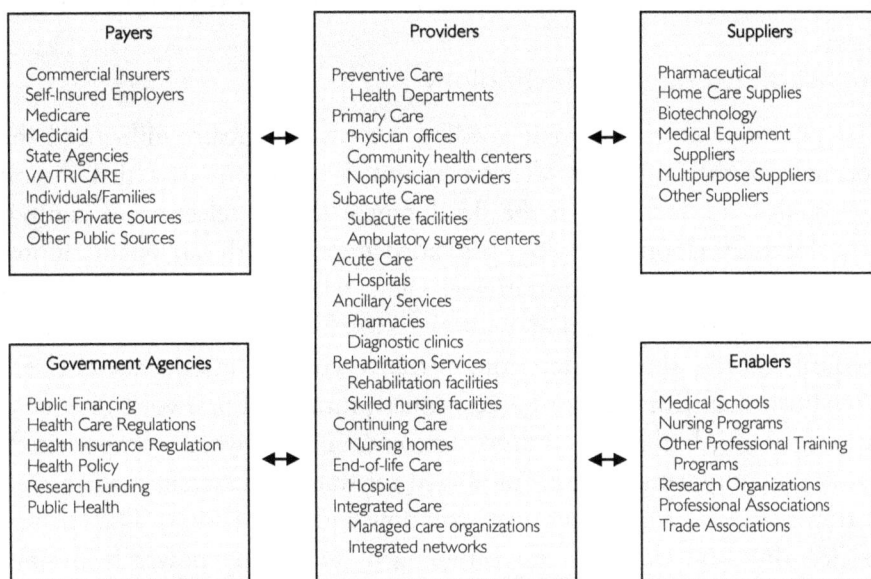

Payers	Providers	Suppliers

Commercial Insurers
Self-Insured Employers
Medicare
Medicaid
State Agencies
VA/TRICARE
Individuals/Families
Other Private Sources
Other Public Sources
	Preventive Care
	  Health Departments
	Primary Care
	  Physician offices
	  Community health centers
	  Nonphysician providers
	Subacute Care
	  Subacute facilities
	  Ambulatory surgery centers
	Acute Care
	  Hospitals
	Ancillary Services
	  Pharmacies
	  Diagnostic clinics
		Pharmaceutical
		Home Care Supplies
		Biotechnology
		Medical Equipment
		  Suppliers
		Multipurpose Suppliers
		Other Suppliers

Government Agencies	Rehabilitation Services	Enablers

Public Financing
Health Care Regulations
Health Insurance Regulation
Health Policy
Research Funding
Public Health
	Rehabilitation facilities
	  Skilled nursing facilities
	Continuing Care
	  Nursing homes
	End-of-life Care
	  Hospice
	Integrated Care
	  Managed care organizations
	  Integrated networks
		Medical Schools
		Nursing Programs
		Other Professional Training
		  Programs
		Research Organizations
		Professional Associations
		Trade Associations

Source: Washington Blue Ribbon Commission, *Health Care Administrative Expense Analysis: Blue Ribbon Commission Recommendation 6 Final Report*, (Olympia, WA: State of Washington Office of Insurance Commissioner, 2007), 11.

Information regarding evaluations from diagnostic studies or referrals to other health professionals can be at various levels of completion or the results can be entered on an entirely separate information technology system. Little or no communication between several health care professionals involved in the care of an individual is a contributing factor to the fragmentation of health care. This leads to a lack of coordinated planning and shared information for follow-ups to monitor improvement or detect early signs of additional problems. Duplication of service is more likely to occur when information sharing among service providers is lacking. Support or referrals to community resources can be overlooked as a result of providers feeling rushed, with barely enough time to address the pressing reason for the visit. Lack of care coordination and/or adequate explanation/clarification of the medical plan of care often results in an emergency room visit or hospitalization. In addition, insufficient support for individual needs of a health care consumer with complex chronic illness can result in the same outcome.

Impact of Information Technology

The introduction of electronic medical records has greatly influenced the operation of the health care delivery system. The manner in which clinical stakeholders are included in the development and/or selection of components for information technology has varied among health care organizations.

Dependence on administrative elements was created to support information technology operation with the switch from paper to electronic medical records, thus adding administrative costs. Clinical personnel are often frustrated with password access issues (number of passwords, frequency of password change, and/or difference in password composition), training requirements for new or altered software, and system malfunction or down time, which impact their workflow and productivity. The reliance of electronics on electricity for on-going or recharging power is another critical issue. Organizations must decide whether to deal with down time when a power outage occurs or to invest in resources for back-up power.

The issues surrounding the use of information technology in the delivery of health care are: (1) how much time providers need to adequately document an interaction with a health care consumer; (2) how information can be shared with other providers outside the system; and (3) how the information can be organized so that specific data can be easily obtained. Computers are not the problem; the problem lies in the application of the technology.[1] The outcome of integrated information technology for an organization should be facilitated workflow, not a more cumbersome one, and the improved availability of quality (clear, concise) communication, not quantity.

The potential value of health information technology is undisputed. It is essential that all organization members maintain a beneficial perspective with development, selection, and implementation of information technology into a health care organization. From Champus and Greenspun's perspective, information technology should be implemented as a part of a re-engineering process rather than for the sake of information technology.[2] "Value to consumers is often lost in a desire to have sophisticated and innovative technology. Best in class capabilities are enablers but not solutions for effective consumerism.[3]

Seth Cohen et al. emphasize four principles for stakeholders in health information technology to achieve consumer-centered care:

1. Keep consumer at the center of innovation.
2. Keep it simple.
3. Invest in a bridge, not an island.
4. Encourage health in addition to treating illness.[4]

"Providers should insure that any single investment in innovation allow for connectivity and information alignment with other settings. The integration of information is critical to ensure the innovators and implementers think about health care the way consumers do."[5]

Organization Expense Management Issues

Transformation in the financial infrastructure is a needed change in the health care system. Significant overhead costs can be seen in each of the health care system components.

Some believe the total administrative costs could be as high as 50 percent when general administration costs of organizations, estimated to be 20 percent, are added to the cost of administering health insurance, estimated to be 30 percent.[6] The lack of a uniform accounting method creates a problem for evaluating true organizational administrative costs. Even though there is no known consensus on what administrative costs actually are, it is apparent this is an area for improvement in cost control within an organization and, in general, the health care system.

Government or private organization mandates and standards of care, such as the Agency for Healthcare Research and Quality (AHRQ) and the Joint Commission on Accreditation of Healthcare Organization (JCAHO), add to administrative costs for policy development and monitoring. Clinical personnel are often required to implement these administrative policies and prepare reports for specific parameters being monitored. These administrative tasks take away clinical time available for interactions with health care consumers.

The income generators for an organization are the health care providers. They often feel they are expected to do more with less and less time allotted per visit, such as implement expanded or new clinical guidelines for numerous conditions in addition to the administrative policy requirements. At times, a health care provider may feel counseling for health behaviors is doing what is right, but it often comes without adequate reimbursement or allotted time.[7,] Adequate reimbursement for preventive care measures to invest in future health status is only part of the issue. Proper reimbursement is also lacking for time doing essential non-visit care planning and coordination. Many reimbursement issues are in the process of review to address adequate accessibility to Patient-Centered Medical Home activities.

Illness Care in the Limelight – A Target for Change

Illness care encompasses acute and chronic care interactions for any health care setting – from a consumer's home to facility-based setting such as an emergency room or hospital. Any deviation from health that needs health care provider interaction falls into the category of illness.

Drivers for the cost of illness care are the medical providers who request diagnostic procedures and testing as well as indicate the follow-up schedule and write out referrals to other medical and ancillary professionals for evaluation and treatment. The cost of illness care is influenced by a health care organization to pay for technology and equipment as well as commercial elements that market pharmaceuticals.[8,] Additionally, higher-cost specialist care is emphasized to evaluate and treat any degree of illness. By contrast, primary care is promoted under the Patient-Centered Medical Home to provide continuity of care at a lower cost and is thus a more efficient approach. It should be noted that a health care consumer with an unstable, uncontrolled chronic condition may be best served under the care of a specialist, at least until stability is established. Information about the health care consumer and medical plan should be communicated, however, to a primary care provider for coordination of services and to maintain the whole person concept.

Prevalence of Chronic Disease

Chronic illnesses have replaced infectious and communicable diseases as leading causes of disease morbidity (number of occurrences) and mortality (number of deaths) and account for the largest portion of health care costs. Nearly 1 in 2 adults, or about 133 million Americans, live with at least one chronic condition.[9,] "Chronic diseases are the most common and costly of all health problems, but they are also the most preventable. Four common, health-damaging, but modifiable behaviors – tobacco use, insufficient physical activity, poor eating habits and excessive alcohol use – are responsible for much of the illness, disability and premature death related to chronic diseases."[10,] It is well demonstrated that risk reduction, chronic disease self-management, and high consumer confidence reduce health care costs by as much as 20 percent.[11,]

The current health care delivery system has made great strides in technological advancements and treatment modalities to combat disease processes. On the other hand, much time, effort, and money are spent in the diagnostic and treatment processes with little effect on the general health of the population. Several years back an article written by Lawrence Green offered an excellent illustration of the problem:

> *There I am standing by the shore of a swiftly flowing river and I hear a cry of a drowning man. So I jump into the river, put my arms around him, pull him to shore and apply artificial respiration. Just when he begins to breathe, there is another cry for help. So I jump into the river, reach him, pull him to shore, apply artificial respiration, and then just as he begins to breathe, another cry for help. So back in the river again, reaching, pulling, applying, breathing and then another yell. Again and again, without end, goes the sequence. You know, I am so busy jumping in, pulling them to shore, applying artificial respiration, that I have no time to see who the hell is upstream pushing them all in.*[12,]

The frustrations and complex issues confronting health care providers as illustrated in Green's article have resonated over the last two decades.

Measures Aimed at Disease Management

The Chronic Care Model[13,] developed by Ed Wagner, MD, and his colleagues at the MacColl Institute for Healthcare Improvement in 1996 has provided a widely used comprehensive framework to manage the care of chronic disease. This model is a guide to higher-quality chronic illness management within primary care.

> *The Chronic Care Model predicts that improvement in its six interrelated components – self-management support, clinical information systems, delivery system redesign, decision support, health care organization, and community resources – can produce system reform in which informed, activated patients interact with prepared, proactive practice teams.*[14,]

In 2001 the faculty staff at the Institute of Healthcare Improvement started investigating office practice settings on-site to detect methods to improve access and efficiency beyond the Chronic Care Model. A key finding of the faculty staff's investigation was that in successful practice settings each health care consumer had a plan of care. The Planned Care Model was subsequently developed with this finding placed at the center of the model. Additional key elements of the Planned Care Model are a care team approach, health care consumer participation, a clinical information system that supports the care team as well as the health care consumer, and organizational leadership that supports all elements of the model.[15,] Details of the development of the Planned Care Model are available in *Innovations in Planned Care.*[16,]

Disease management and population management programs can be created for the benefit of tracking the status of given parameters for an individual or group of individuals with the same diagnosis. However, if they work in isolation away from the whole person concept, care is fragmented. Likewise, working with medical plans of care for specific chronic conditions in isolation will likely cause a lack of essential communication links for care coordination, resulting in possible duplication of service and problems with timing of effective interventions.

Change Focus to Preventive Care

Effective measures do exist today to prevent or delay much of the chronic disease burden and curtail its devastating consequences, but those measures have taken a back seat to illness care. Preventive care activities seek to protect health care consumers from potential or actual health threats and their harmful consequences. The U.S. Preventive Services Task Force (USPSTF) is charged with the responsibility to identify evidence-based measures to accomplish this purpose. It is an independent panel of various experts established in 1984 to periodically review and make recommendations on scientific evidence for clinical preventive care, grading the magnitude of net benefit from A (recommends the service) through D (recommends against the service). "I" statements by the Task Force are issued when evidence is insufficient to determine net benefit.[17,]

In his Foreward to *Health Promotion and Disease Prevention in Clinical Practice,* Michael McGinnis identifies the beginning of preventive care as dating back to the B.C. era:

> *From the time that the elements of medicine and health were first recorded, prevention has provided a philosophical and conceptual cornerstone. Some 2500 years ago, Hippocrates penned into the physicians' solemn oath a pledge to help keep patients from harm, and used On Aire and Places to elaborate in detail on the physician's obligation to learn and understand the strong influence of external influences on sickness and disease. [18,]*

Changing the underlying causes of preventable illness conditions will change the demand and cost for illness care as well as benefit the quality of life for individual health care consumers. The main goal of preventive care is to reduce the burden of illness from the major preventable diseases and reduce disability. One important approach is to actively integrate preventive care for screening and early interventions into the medical plan of care to improve outcomes by lessening consequences of disease progression and disability.

Consumer-driven health care (a specific health insurance plan) is presented as one means to reward prevention proactively. Health care consumers make choices about where their funds that have been set aside for their health care are dispersed. "Prevention of illness, injury or associated risk factors is the ultimate *cost-trend mitigation strategy*," according to Dr. Parkinson while in his medical role at a consumer-directed health care plan.[19,] A focus on preventive care can dramatically reduce the long-term cost burden and health care demands of chronic conditions.

Barriers or resistance to preventive care are recognized among health care consumers, providers, and systems. It will be a cognitive change to switch from a downstream (illness) to an upstream (wellness) focus. Health care consumers often are confused by conflicting messages in the media about what services are beneficial. Without symptoms, health care consumers often do not see the investment in prevention measures as being worthwhile, or the consumers may merely lack funds or have other priorities. Health care providers are often trained about acute care over preventive care. They may perceive a lack of time for engaging in preventive care activities or may receive no immediate results with which to evaluate immediate effectiveness. An existing system may be inadequate for determining which preventive service is appropriate for a given individual, which can be in part due to a lack of documentation for what the health care consumer has already received such as immunizations or screening tests.

The problem with lack of reimbursement for preventive care services will be alleviated with the Patient Safety and Affordable Care Act of 2010 (henceforth the Affordable Care Act), providing that provision remains viable in light of the recent U.S. Supreme Court decision to uphold the current law. It currently requires non-grandfathered plans to provide first-dollar coverage (no deductible) for preventive care service starting in 2011 for:

- U.S. Preventive Service Task Force (USPSTF) recommended A or B services only
- Centers for Disease Control and Prevention (CDC) recommended immunizations
- Health Resources and Services Administration (HRSA) preventive care guidelines and screenings for infants, children, and women[20,]

The Dominant Role of Third Party Payers in Transactions for Health Care Services

In a usual and customary transaction to purchase services, individuals use their own money, trying to maximize its value.[21,] Service providers will normally respond by aiming for maximum efficiency for delivery of these services to control costs. However in America, only about 12 percent of health care consumers shop with their own money. In other words, 88 percent of medical bills are paid by the government and private insurance.[22,] Health care consumers are insulated from the cost of the service and do not take price into account when deciding to request the service.

Health Insurance as a Payer for Health Care Services

Health insurance, government or private, is handled by a third party administrator that determines which services are paid and the amount paid for each service. This adds administrative costs to the health insurance plan or program as well as a profit margin for the private insurance sector. The Washington State Blue Ribbon Commission evaluated administrative health care costs in 2007. These costs varied from 12 to 17 percent, depending on the setting. The variance was attributed to the lack of consistency in accounting for administrative costs as previously stated. It is difficult to compare apples to apples when looking at a fruit basket – there is no single set of definitions for various components of administrative expenses nor a consistent tracking method.[23,] The Washington State Blue Ribbon Commission report further stated: "Our analysis indicates that approximately 14 percent of every dollar received by a physician office is devoted to health plan-provider interaction. In addition, the physicians themselves spend up to over two hours per day working on health plan related administrative work."[24,] Hence, the combined cost for administering health insurance at both levels, the insurance company and the office of the physician, was estimated to be as high at 30 percent.[25,]

Connection Lost to Cost and Responsibility

A communication wedge is created between the point of service provider (the clinician) and the consumer (the patient) when a third party enters the transaction to purchase health care services. The health care consumer is relegated to the role of *beneficiary*. The third party payer becomes the actual *customer*. The health care consumer thus experiences a loss of connectivity to the cost and the most efficient utilization of services.

How many health care consumers are aware of the allocation of funds from the premiums paid for their health insurance, whether or not they make a contribution? Hundreds of billions of dollars go into premiums for health insurance plans over which health care consumers often have little or no personal control. In years past, health insurance was basically purchased to cover an unexpected high cost or catastrophic event. The American culture has transitioned to the current perception that health care insurance is required for the delivery of all health care services and expectation for first dollar coverage (no deductible). The Affordable Care Act included a component that the purchase of health insurance will be mandatory unless the U.S. Congress changes that provision following the U.S. Supreme Court ruling to uphold that provision. It reflects the mind-set that health insurance is required to receive all health care services. This mind-set is reinforced when the first question asked when presenting for care is: "Do you have health insurance?"

One could argue that personal health insurance purchased by employers or the government distorts health care consumer sense of personal health responsibility. An inadvertent outcome with third party payer arrangements is the perception that the payer for the health care services becomes responsible for managing health problems. In other words, the employer or government owns the problem of an individual's health care. How does this isolation from direct financial responsibility affect a health care consumer's motivation to prevent downstream health consequences?

Traditionally, funds from health insurance are mixed or pooled for reserve accounts to pay claims. A claim filed for pooled funds disperses financial consequences to all pool donors. There is no direct connection to the amount previously paid in behalf of a health care consumer. The perspective can be created that an unlimited source of funds is available for an individual's needs. For the most part, the concept of health insurance lacks both the expectation of individual responsibility for behavior leading to unfavorable health conditions and the incentive for individuals to prevent an incident. This is not the case for Health Savings Accounts or Consumer-Directed Health Plans (consumer-controlled accounts) where an individual has some control over the spending of their funds.

When health care consumers share in the cost of their purchasing decision, they will be more likely to make those decisions based on price and value.[26,] Insurance to protect against personal financial devastation by a catastrophic event is a rational approach for everyone. Cost control issues are not addressed by merely having health insurance. Awareness of cost and active participation in the purchasing decisions are essential for cost control and efficient utilization of health care services. Third party payers and the absence of individual financial responsibility favor an environment of entitlement and unlimited demand for health care service.[27,] Therefore, would it not be more beneficial for all health care consumers to have a plan for health care or "health plan" whereby a component could be insurance for a catastrophic event?

The Segal Group takes the position that creating consumerism (active participation in selection and payment of service) in the health care industry is considerably more difficult because most health care consumers cannot accurately measure the quality of recommended or competing services. They will often seek a service regardless of its price due to the emotional nature of the purchase decision and their insulation from the true cost.[28,] In other words, health care consumer do not currently have the resources to evaluate the cost and value of a service in relationship to other comparable services. How can the health care consumer get better connected to the cost and value of health care services? The consumer-controlled accounts, Health Savings Accounts or Consumer-Directed Health Plans, surfaced to improve awareness of cost of services and control over purchasing decisions. They set the stage for consumers to think of purchasing health care as spending their own money and making an effort to spend it wisely. Michael Parkinson,

MD, Chief Health and Medical Officer at Lumenos, firmly states: "Empowering health care consumers financially and educationally can decrease the administrative hassles dealt by both the consumers and provider as well as getting other stakeholders out of the exam room."[29,] Changing the role of third party payers will over time leave the personal decisions to health care consumers and providers.[30,]

Countless studies have been conducted to ascertain why the American health care system does not have the outcomes commensurate with cost. A plausible explanation could be the service connection between health care consumer and provider has too many intermediaries and/or there is a distortion of accountability for one's daily health choices when others pay for related health services.

Notes

1. Jim Champy and Harry Greenspun. *Reengineering Health Care: A Manifesto for Radically Rethinking Health Care Delivery* (Upper Saddle River, NJ: Pearson Education, 2010), 3.

2. Jim Champy and Harry Greenspun. *Reengineering Health Care: A Manifesto for Radically Rethinking Health Care Delivery* (Upper Saddle River, NJ: Pearson Education, 2010), 80.

3. Seth Cohen and others. "Increasing Consumerism in Healthcare through Intelligent Information Technology," *The American Journal of Managed Care* 16, Special Edition (2010), SP41.

4. Seth Cohen and others. "Increasing Consumerism in Healthcare through Intelligent Information Technology," *The American Journal of Managed Care* 16, Special Edition (2010), SP41-SP42.

5. Seth Cohen and others. "Increasing Consumerism in Healthcare through Intelligent Information Technology," *The American Journal of Managed Care* 16, Special Edition (2010), SP 41.

6. Washington Blue Ribbon Commission, *Health Care Administrative Expense Analysis: Blue Ribbon Commission Recommendation 6 Final Report* (Olympia, WA: Washington State Office of Insurance Commissioner, 2007), 3.

7. Steven H. Woolf, Steven Jonas, and Evonne Kaplan-Liss. *Health Promotion and Disease Prevention in Clinical Practice,* 2nd ed. (Philadelphia, PA: Lippincott Williams and Wilkins, 2008), xxxv.

8. James F. Fries and others. "Beyond Health Promotion: Reducing Need and Demand for Medical Care," *Health Affairs* 17, no. 2 (1998): 75.

9. Centers for Disease Control and Prevention (CDC). "Chronic Diseases: The Power to Prevent; The Call to Control" National Center for Chronic Disease Prevention and Health Promotion (2009), 2, *http://www.cdc.gov/chronicdisease/resources/publications/AAG/pdf/chronic.pdf* (accessed July 3, 2012).

10. Centers for Disease Control and Prevention (CDC). "Chronic Diseases: The Power to Prevent; The Call to Control" National Center for Chronic Disease Prevention and Health Promotion (2009), 2, *http://www.cdc.gov/chronicdisease/resources/publications/AAG/pdf/chronic.pdf* (accessed July 3, 2012).

11. James F. Fries and others. "Beyond Health Promotion: Reducing Need and Demand for Medical Care." *Health Affairs* 17, no. 2 (1998): 71.

12. Lawrence W. Green. "Health Promotion Policy and the Placement of Responsibility for Personal Health Care."*Family and Community Health* 3, no. 3 (1979): 51.

13. Andrea I. Kabcenell, Jerry Langley, and Cindy Hupke. *Innovations in Planned Care. IHI Innovation Series White Papers.* (Cambridge, MA: Institute for Healthcare Improvement, 2006), 4.

14. Thomas Bodenheimer, Edward H. Wagner, and Kevin Grumbach. "Improving Primary Care for Patients with Chronic Illness." *JAMA* 288, no.14 (2002): 1775.

15. Andrea I. Kabcenell, Jerry Langley, and Cindy Hupke. *Innovations in Planned Care. IHI Innovation Series White Papers.* (Cambridge, MA: Institute for Healthcare Improvement, 2006), 8.

16. Andrea I. Kabcenell, Jerry Langley, and Cindy Hupke. *Innovations in Planned Care. IHI Innovation Series White Papers.* (Cambridge, MA: Institute for Healthcare Improvement, 2006), 8-15.

17. Tricia Trinite, Carol Loveland-Cherry, and Lucy Marion. "The U.S. Preventive Service Task Force: An Evidence-Based Preventive Resource for Nurse Practitioners." *Journal of American Academy of Nurse Practitioners* 21, (2009): 302.

18. Michael McGinnis. "Forward" in Woolf et al *Health Promotion and Disease Prevention in Clinical Practice,* 2nd ed. (Philadelphia, PA: Lippincott Williams and Wilkins, 2008), vii.

19. Michael D. Parkinson. *Consumer-Driven Healthcare: Prevention, Evidence-Based Care and Better Patient-Physician Relationships.* (Alexandria, VA: Lumenos, n.d.), 1, *http://www.acpm.org/resource/resmgr/perpectives-files/perspectives_Consumer_Driven.pdf* (accessed June 20, 2012).

20. National Business Group on Health. *Payment Systems, Government Policies and Market Incentives Should Refocus Efforts on Disease Prevention.* (Washington, DC, 2010), 1, *http://www.businessgrouphealth.org/pdfs/preventioncarepositionstatement.pdf* (accessed June 20, 2012).

21. Doug Mataconis. *Health Care Costs and the Third Party Payer Problem* (2011), 5, *http://www.outsidethebeltway.com/health-care-costs-and-the-third-party-payer-problem/* (accessed February 10, 2012).

22. Centers for Medicare and Medicaid Services (CMS). *The Nation's Health Dollar, Calendar Year 2010: Where It Came From.* Office of the Actuary National Health Statistics Group (Baltimore, MD: U.S. Department of Health and Human Services), 1.

23. Washington Blue Ribbon Commission. *Health Care Administrative Expense Analysis: Blue Ribbon Commission Recommendation 6 Final Report* (Olympia, WA: Washington State Office of Insurance Commissioner, 2007), 10.

24. Washington Blue Ribbon Commission. *Health Care Administrative Expense Analysis: Blue Ribbon Commission Recommendation 6 Final Report* (Olympia, WA: Washington State Office of Insurance Commissioner, 2007), 3.

25. Washington Blue Ribbon Commission. *Health Care Administrative Expense Analysis: Blue Ribbon Commission Recommendation 6 Final Report* (Olympia, WA: Washington State Office of Insurance Commissioner, 2007), 3.

26. Doug Mataconis. *Health Care Costs and the Third Party Payer Problem* (2011), 1, *http://www.outsidethebeltway.com/health-care-costs-and-the-third-party-payer-problem/* (accessed February 10, 2012).

27. Center for Health Transformation. Healthcare Consumerism: The Basis of a 21st Century Intelligent Health System (2006), 2, *http://www.healthcarevisions.net/f/2006_Healthcare_ Consumerism_CHT.pdf* (accessed June 20, 2012).

28. The Segal Group. Consumerism in Health Care: The Quest to Create New Partnerships for Responsibility and Accountability, an Executive Letter from The Segal Company (2003), 1.

29. Michael D. Parkinson. *Consumer-Driven Healthcare: Prevention, Evidence-Based Care and Better Patient-Physician Relationships.* (Alexandria, VA: Lumenos, n.d.), 3, *http://www.acpm.org/resource/resmgr/perpectives-files/ perspectives_Consumer_Driven.pdf* (accessed June 20, 2012).

30. Michael D. Parkinson. *Consumer-Driven Healthcare: Prevention, Evidence-Based Care and Better Patient-Physician Relationships.* (Alexandria, VA: Lumenos, n.d.), 3, *http://www.acpm.org/resource/resmgr/perpectives-files/ perspectives_Consumer_ Driven.pdf* (accessed June 20, 2012).

Chapter Three

A Discussion on DIRECTED CARE –
Setting the Stage for Better Health Care Consumer Utilization Patterns

The concept of DIRECTED CARE evolved from a desire to look at the health care system from the consumers' perspective. They have been nudged from their individual "customer" role, loosing the usual and customary service connection to their health care provider. Generally, their feelings of being frustrated and overwhelmed are overlooked in the current health care delivery process. Depersonalized health care services become merely billing information and statistical reports.

In the prevailing milieu, the business of medicine is forcing the art of medicine and nursing to wane to a barely detectable level. It appears the health care system has gotten the cart before the horse with emphasis on payment rather than the way the health care consumer utilizes the system. Most Americans are on the receiving end of decisions made by third party payers, leaving them as individuals without direct control over the dollars that finance health benefits or medical care. A re-engineered system should also include measures to reconnect the health care consumers to value and cost of services they receive.

The present challenge is to design and implement a system that delivers excellent preventive care and treatment when required for all health care consumers across all diseases processes. Doing this just for health care consumers with chronic disease or for only one condition at a time may be feasible but not sustainable from a service or financial perspective.[1] The Institute for Health Improvement proposes the following considerations for a better system, considerations that formed the basis for their Planned Care Model:

- All health care consumers need a customized plan for prevention and treatment of medical conditions.
- Effective care for health care consumers with multiple conditions cannot be sustained if care systems and guidelines are just added one on top of the other.
- Self-care management skills help health care consumers to function better and maintain well-being, regardless of their capacity or condition. Efforts to develop these skills for every health care consumer need to be built into the delivery system.
- Care for health care consumers with chronic conditions is most effective when office visits are combined with non-visit care; yet current payment systems generally cover only office-based care.
- Information about health care consumers must be available to all providers that the consumers encounter in their communities.[2]

Consumer-directed or person-directed care (not same as consumer-directed health care insurance plan) has been used in community-based settings, working under the premise that individuals with impairments remain knowledgeable about their own needs and can make choices that work best for them. Professional nurses play an active role in these settings to promote maximum self-sufficiency. Why not expand the concept for application in ambulatory primary care aimed toward health care consumers making improved decisions for utilization of health care services and self-management skills for optimal wellness? In this application, DIRECTED CARE is defined within the context that to direct means to point out or guide, to instruct, or to manage.[3] Therefore, DIRECTED CARE will be defined as:

the use of professional nursing expertise to guide health care consumers down pathways of effective and efficient utilization of health care resources and to influence their personal health behaviors toward optimal wellness.

The Rationale

Conceptually, health care *need* is poorly defined and may be used interchangeably with *want*, *desire*, or *demand*. Health care consumers may not always be able to clearly express their needs and/or the provider may find it difficult to assess the intensity of different needs. For the purpose of presenting the concept of DIRECTED CARE, all definitions of health care need are put in the context of demand management or consumer utilization of services.

Variability in individual health care consumer demand has been linked to the presence or absence of consumer confidence and to the availability of reliable, valid information to guide health care consumers to make the most appropriate decisions.[4] DIRECTED CARE strategies focus on providing information and support to health care consumers to empower them to manage minor health problems and make appropriate use of acute and chronic care services. Successfully implementing DIRECTED CARE will require shifting from a downstream focus on illness care to an upstream focus that includes preventive care with health promotion and disease prevention activities. The transition will not be simple, easy, or immediate, but will incur the same issues as with any change – a feeling of discomfort and unfamiliarity.

Managing Utilization of Health Care Resources

Demand management is based on the principle that, given the right information and support, health care consumers are the best managers of their own health. This principle hinges on health care consumers taking responsibility for their health. Appropriate self-care and self-management is preferred to professional care when health care consumers, provided with relevant information, can determine when professional care is required.[5]

Multiple studies have demonstrated that providing health care consumers with information and guidance for self-management can lower health care service utilization by 7 to 17 percent, at very low cost when compare to the cost of other professional encounters.[6] James Fries, MD, Stanford School of Medicine professor, was an advocate for the concept of demand management in the 1990s and wrote numerous articles clarifying that demand management (consumer side) is unlike managed care (provider side) in that it does not withhold treatment or limit access. Conceptually, demand management has been visualized as improving access and decreasing costs because only those consumers who really need medical care will seek it out. More recent articles address this same concept as consumerism and discuss utilization of health care services based on the same principles.

Health care utilization patterns have not significantly changed in the past decade. The demand for on-going illness care has resulted in a high rate of utilization of extensive resources for chronic care. As previously discussed, management of chronic disease is a large contributory factor to health care costs. The Planned Care Model will help utilization management of resources and provide better chronic care outcomes if implemented by health care providers..

American health care consumers need to understand their role and responsibilities to minimize their demand for health care services and resulting cost. The reconnection of health care consumers to the cost of the service transactions is also necessary for cost containment. Optimally, the health care consumer will also have an opportunity to control components of their health plan and payment for services.

The Role of Professional Nurses

Why position professional nurses on point for this concept of care? First of all, the nursing profession has the largest segment in the health care workforce. Professional nurses are a human resource well-qualified to take the reins for DIRECTED CARE. However, today they can be found in roles where their expertise is underutilized or is utilized more in clerical roles than for assessment or synthesizing data. Professional nurses excel in facilitating communication, synthesizing data, advising/consulting, and providing information and support to increase health care consumers' abilities and confidence in self-management skills. These professional nurse skills form the cornerstones for DIRECTED CARE interactions.

The American Nurses Association (ANA) provides a comprehensive definition of professional nursing as: *"the protection, promotion, and optimization of health and abilities, prevention of illness and injury, alleviation of suffering through the diagnosis and treatment of human response, and advocacy in the care of individuals, families, communities, and populations.*[7] The professional nursing roles in promoting health and coordinating care can be seen as prominent aspects for nursing practice throughout the ANA's Nursing Scope and Standards of Practice (See Appendix B) and in the Nurse Practitioner Primary Care Competencies, written jointly by the American Association of Colleges of Nursing (AACN) and the National Organization of Nurse Practitioner Faculties (NONPF).[8]

The promotion of health is a well-known independent practice component of professional nurses' roles, including advanced practice. The World Health Organization (WHO) defines health promotion as: *"the process of enabling people to increase control over their health and its determinants, and thereby improve their health."*[9] The central goal of health promotion is to improve personal health behaviors and ultimately to delay or prevent onset of disease by reduction in risk factors. This will have a long-term effect on health care utilization of services. Professional nurses can take a proactive stance to realign and solidify a focus on health promotion and disease prevention.

The qualifications of the nurse practitioner include an expanded knowledge base and expertise in assessment and intervention options for the physical and psychological dimensions of an individual's health. Nurse practitioners have received extended formal education for accessing and developing a management plan to maximize an individual's health potential. In DIRECTED CARE, nurse practitioners will work in tandem with registered nurses and will be a valuable contribution to team-based services. The degree of synthesis of information and specific scope of practice capabilities make the nurse practitioner a valued team member for wellness care. Specific role responsibilities for health or wellness care include conducting age- and gender-specific health maintenance evaluations (HME): (1) requesting screening tests; (2) prescribing immunizations and chemophylaxis; (3) assisting with integration of a health monitoring plan; (4) providing information about the consequences of unhealthy personal behavior; and (5) setting priorities for care management. It is recognized that nurse practitioners may be placed in the position of concurrent wellness and illness provider roles. However, an intent of the DIRECTED CARE discussion is to establish a justification for more nurse practitioner time in wellness care. As with all other team-based members, consulting/advising or coaching/supporting personal health behavior changes is an on-going activity for nurse practitioners.

The excellence demonstrated by professional nurses in leadership, coordination of care, and health consultation is not new. Their ability to coordinate and orchestrate multidimensional hospitalized care for full 24-hour time periods has long been recognized. Home Health entered the health care system, and once again nurses took the lead to outline and coordinate care for health care consumer needs in a specific setting. It should not be a surprise that the ambulatory care setting presents an opportunity for professional nurses to step forward again in a redefined role and become independent care leaders and consultants. Guiding a health care consumer to the right place, at the right time, and with the right provider will impact the way the consumer utilizes the health care system.

As presented in the Institute of Medicine (IOM) 2010 report, *The Future of Nursing: Leading Change, Advancing Health* , the close contact of professional nurses with health care consumers and other professionals, as well as their scientific understanding of the care continuum, provides nurses with a unique ability to lead improvement and re-engineering of the health care system.[10] In addition, with the art of nursing being framed around caring and respect for human dignity,[11] DIRECTED CARE becomes a great fit for professional nurses.

DIRECTED CARE is one aspect of a team-based care coordination and care management by professional nurses performing autonomously within the full scope of nursing practice. Professional nurses will take the lead for wellness care aimed at health care consumers "getting healthy and staying healthy." The IOM report, cited in the previous paragraph, summarizes the contribution of professional nurses to meet the challenges in a re-engineered health care system, converting to patient-centered care and primary care as opposed to specialty care:

"Nurses are well poised to meet these needs by virtue of their numbers, scientific knowledge and adaptive capacity, and health care organizations would benefit from taking advantage of the contributions nurses can make."[12]

Linking to a Patient-Centered Medical Home

The first major improvement in an effort to re-engineer the health care system is the continued evolution of the Patient-Centered Medical Home (PCMH). This movement is enhanced by the provisions of the Affordable Care Act, which supports PCMH expansion. The Patient-Centered Medical Home represents a viable coordinated care model with health care consumers sharing the decision making about all aspects of their care. Health care provider adherence to the PCMH Joint Principles should demonstrate a marked improvement in continuity of care and action plans constructed with health care consumer input. The Patient-Centered Medical Home model promotes active participation of health care consumers and shared care management with providers, which will require collaboration within the medical community. Health care consumers are brought back to the forefront in their service consumer role. For PCMH to succeed, the clinical side of health care services must be allowed to resurface as the dominant management process with administration elements in a support role in lieu of overshadowing clinical services.

The Patient-Centered Medical Home would make a great union with DIRECTED CARE. Blending these concepts builds an integrated summary of data and is directed toward optimal utilization of the health care system focused on health promotion and disease prevention. The intent is to establish a shared wellness/illness care management relationship over time with health care providers and consumers.

Moving Preventive Care to the Forefront as an Offensive Strategy

Promoting health and preventing disease has inherent logic. It seems more reasonable to prevent disease from occurring or forestalling the process of pathogenesis than waiting until irreversible damage has occurred to the body. Why wait until diabetic retinopathy claims eyesight? Is it not more reasonable to instill effective chronic care management for diabetes to minimize the risk of blindness at the earliest stage? Another excellent example is the epidemic of obesity, even among children. One third of Americans adults are obese. Obese young people number one in every five among ages 6 to 19.[13] Obesity is projected to replace smoking as the leading cause of preventable death in the near future.[14] The downstream impact of obesity is clearly documented in the literature by increasing risk for diabetes, cardiovascular disease, and joint conditions. The day-to-day life of an obese person is burdened with decreased work productivity and decreased well-being. It seems rational and logical to place promoting healthy food choices and/or interactions about current body mass index (BMI) on the agenda for every preventive care visit.

This illustration makes the case that it is economical to stay healthy.

Health promotion and maintenance are preferable to the current focus on high-tech costly illness care.

Reproduced by permission from Elsevier-Mosby for Elizabeth F. Wywialowski, *Managing Client Care*, 3rd ed. (St. Louis, MO: Mosby, 2004), 38.

The target for DIRECTED CARE health promotion and disease prevention activities is: (1) to reduce the burden of illness for the major preventable diseases and (2) to increase the health care consumers' awareness of the need to maintain and/or to improve their health status. It is believed that individual-based interactions will benefit the development of collaborated strategies for health care consumers to "get healthy and stay healthy." An emphasis on health promotion and disease prevention will impact the utilization patterns of health care consumers in a positive way.

The natural history of disease was described in *Preventive Medicine for the Doctor in His Community* in 1965.[15] Adaptations of Leavell and Clark's diagram illustrating the progression of natural history of disease can be seen even today in the literature and health care educational curriculum for discussions about levels of prevention. Table 3.1 is one of these adaptations and shows how the preventive care focus alters as the health status changes and the disease process escalates, resulting in increased suffering and cost.

Table 3.1.   Relating Preventive Care to Progression of Disease or Injury

Dimensions of Preventive Care				
Health				Disease
Prepathogenesis Period		Period of Pathogenesis		
Low Cost				High Cost
Primary Prevention		Secondary Prevention		Tertiary Prevention
Health Promotion	Specific Protection	Early Diagnosis	Prompt and Adequate Treatment	Rehabilitation and Disability Limitation

Adapted from: Hugh R. Leavell and E. Gurney Clark. *Preventive Medicine for the Doctor in His Community*, 2nd ed. (New York: McGraw-Hill. 1965), 28.

Prevention is a more rational strategy than dealing with disease at any age. Efforts exerted on all three levels of preventive care are important components of all health promotion and disease prevention programs. Health promotion should be considered for its long-term health effects, since it does not provide the immediate results that are often seen with symptom relief. "Available data suggests a minimum lag period of two to three years between improvement in health habits and better health and reduced costs."[16] Thus, the benefits of changing one's behavior are not immediately noticed.

DIRECTED CARE is geared toward an upstream approach to promote health and prevent disease through all three levels of preventive care in collaboration with the health care consumer and other team-based members.

1. *Primary prevention* aims to prevent risk factors for disease through health promotion primarily through information sharing relative to circumstances.
2. *Secondary prevention* works to identify and detect disease in its earliest stage through specified screening tests.
3. *Tertiary prevention* involves actual treatment of disease to limit complications and disabilities associated with a specific disease and to restore self-sufficiency.

Appendices C, D, and E illustrate disease prevention, injury prevention, and mental health issues respectively across the spectrum of preventive care.

Personal health behaviors that cause disease play a key etiologic role early in the time line presented above. Modification of personal health behaviors early in the natural history of disease (pathogenesis) has the potential to prevent or reverse, in some circumstances, the progression of the disease process. Early intervention by modification of health behavior can be effective even before a disease process is detectable by a screening test or physical evaluation. A disease process must have produced a detectable pathophysiologic abnormality before screening tests are useful.[17]

The most difficult barriers to overcome in health care delivery for prospective preventive care will be the lack of health care consumer understanding of preventive care benefits and the entrenched position of the health care system in the retrospective illness-focused care that it has held for decades. Woolf et al. describe the problem confronting health care providers to address prevention in their day-to-day office practice. Providers are reluctant to emphasize personal health behaviors and other risk factors during illness care visits. Health care providers are accustomed to dealing with the here-and-now, real pathology scenarios. Additionally, the emphasis has been on testing rather than talking due to a perception that screening tests are more effective than counseling.[18]

Changing the health care system to bring preventive care to the forefront will require a long transition period before all aspects are engaged. It is essential that all members of the team-based Patient-Centered Medical Home consistently promote and encourage upstream health care consumer actions. Changing the underlying cause of preventable disease will change the demand and cost for illness care as well as benefit the quality of life for individual health care consumers.

Increasing Access to Communication with Health Care Professionals

Health care consumers seek interactions with health professionals to obtain information or to identify a health issue and receive treatment. They visualize their providers as the most credible sources on health matters. Health care consumers have cited advice from health care providers as an important reason for their success in changing a behavior.[19]

It is important to set the stage for health care consumers to speak up to state their preferences, to express opinions if uncomfortable with something, or to ask questions if they do not understand something.[20] A favorable environment allows health care consumers to tell their stories and ask questions. An article linking the health care consumer and provider communication to health outcomes cites research that reports communication centered on health care consumers leads to mutually agreed upon plans of care that work best for the consumer and help them to stay committed to that plan, ultimately leading to better health outcomes.[21] Therefore, an approach that respects health care consumers' own values and circumstances is necessary for them to become engaged in self-management for themselves or their children and to make informed decisions.

From the above perspective, all information sharing and coaching/supporting activities need to be converted to individualized approaches. Passive instruction (telling) or merely providing handouts to health care consumers lacks evidence of subsequent improvement in health care consumers' self-management or any measurable impact on long-term outcomes.[22] As an example of passive instruction, millions of self-care books were distributed during the 1990s to American households through employers or health care plans to provide medical self-help to their employees and beneficiaries. These books outlined actions to take through algorithms (decision trees) based on presenting symptoms. The missing link was an opportunity to interact with a health care professional to ask questions to help clarify the content or rationale for the instructions. Having access to self-care instructions (written or computer-based) for acute self-limiting conditions is important. However, an evaluation of an individual health care consumer's skill and confidence to use the material is also needed. If an individual does not comprehend the material, it will probably not be used. Another issue is that the information needs to be relevant to that individual. A single, healthy adult is not likely to access information for acute (first-aid) issues when chronic care issues are intermixed or presented just as a volume of information for all men, women, and children. Printed information or computer-based programs need to have readily accessible information related to age, gender, and specific health inquiry or need.

Communication between the provider and health care consumer will greatly impact outcomes. A paternalistic communication approach is one in which a provider acts as a parent, placing the health care consumer in a dependent, child-like role. The communication in this type of interaction is seen as a "talking to" approach. A non-compliant label is attached if the health care consumer does not follow instructions. On the other hand, the "communicating with" approach places attention on the health issue from the health care consumer's perspective, including addressing their fears and values.

Effective communication in a "patient-centered" approach includes developing a common shared understanding of the problem or illness, addressing the health care consumer's feelings, beliefs, expectations and concerns, knowing the "whole person" as well as their family and social context, and collaboratively choosing among options for treatment, behavior change and follow-up.[23]

Health care providers must recognize that change has to come from within themselves to overcome the pull on them toward the traditional "fix-it" role. Merely telling the health care consumer what to do has traditionally been the method of instruction for a medical plan of care as well as health education and counseling. Health care providers who find themselves stuck in the traditional "telling" approach need to make a transition from didactic lecturer to facilitator, helping the health care consumer work through a life-change process. In that new role, the health care provider clarifies the consumers' thoughts and expectations, and identifies their source of resistance, pointing out inconsistencies and correcting misconceptions.[24] Listening skills of the health professionals are essential for this type of communication.

The value of effective communication and building relationships with health care consumers was well summarized on a *No Time to Teach* blog:

Sharing information is just the beginning of the process. We then need to help patients and families fit these new treatments and behaviors into their lives, and find a new balance, a new way of living. This process involves the whole interdisciplinary health care team, across the continuity of care, over time. The bad news is, it's not a quick fix. The good news: it works and saves money by preventing costly medical problems.[25]

Building the Foundation for DIRECTED CARE

DIRECTED CARE draws on attributes of several concepts: Orem's Self-Care Nursing Model,[26] case management, Planned Care Model,[27] coordinated care, Health Belief Model,[28] Situational Leadership Model,[29] empowerment, summary record, health coaching, motivational interviewing, and consumerism. All professional nurses will practice independently in health promotion for primary preventive care. Nurse practitioners will provide preventive care within their scope of practice for secondary and tertiary prevention levels. Planning and coordinating clinic visits with preventive care incorporated, increasing health care consumers' skill and confidence in making health care decisions, and coaching for healthy personal behavior will decrease need and demand for medical services.

Professional nurses, both registered and advanced practice, become the optimal team-based providers for DIRECTED CARE, working with health care consumers over time to identify and minimize health risks and to assist health care consumers to become confident decision makers for appropriate utilization of health care resources. Table 3.2 below summarizes the rationale for DIRECTED CARE activities by professional nurses.

Table 3.2. System Re-engineering Strategies Engaging Professional Nursing Expertise

Target	Strategies	Specific Proactive/Prospective Actions
Decrease system complexity	• Guide health care consumers through navigation of the health care system. • Inject clinical team input and control into delivery of health care services to support efficient use of • provider time and continuity of care. • Create a system with flexibility to accommodate characteristics of population served by a primary care practice.	• Collaborate with medical providers to integrate medical plan of care for each chronic condition for annual Health Monitoring Plan . • Provide consulting and coaching to increase health care consumer ability and confidence in health care system navigation. • Develop Summary Health Care Record for each health care consumer. • Position professional nurses to assume independent responsibility for orchestrating workflow for wellness care. • Re-engineer electronic health information system to minimize provider time to enter or seek information when warranted.

Target	Strategies	Specific Proactive/Prospective Actions
Restructure health care system with emphasis on preventive care - primary, secondary, tertiary.	• Reduce need and demand for reactive/retrospective illness care. • Redirect emphasis to wellness and construct outcomes to reflect direction toward getting healthy, staying healthy.	• Conduct annual Wellness Checks. • Evaluate health risks annually. • Counsel health care consumers for at-risk personal health behaviors and anticipatory guidance appropriate for age and gender. • Provide self-care advice and coaching for minor injuries and diseases. • Provide advice and coaching for self-management of chronic conditions. • Select annual health promotion theme for general population.
Improve communication and/or connection to health care provider.	• Promote health care consumer active participation in decision making for health care services. • Increase health care consumer confidence and ability in problem identification and resolution. • Provide feedback on correlation between actual utilization and health monitoring plan.	• Design planned visits for preventive and chronic care. • Develop integrated Health Monitoring Plan. • Conduct annual utilization review for each health care consumer. • Support consumer-directed care. • Engage health care consumer in scheduling and coordinating reimbursement for services. • Make nursing consultation (triage) available 24/7 to manage acute episodes in accordance with telehealth nursing standards and approved physician protocol. • Establish communication mechanism for follow-up to surgical procedures, emergency visits, and hospitalization as well as any medical interventions obtained outside primary care.

DIRECTED CARE is foreseen as an embedded component of the Patient-Centered Medical Home (PCMH), an optimal location for providing services. This relationship will enhance the platform for establishing the whole person plan of care by integrating preventive care and promoting a heightened skill level for health care consumers in making health care decisions. However, it is not essential that DIRECTED CARE be attached to a PCMH, but it should be attached to some form of team-based care. It is essential not to establish a silo effect in which professional nurses perform independent activities in isolation and thus create fragmented care.

Quality of care occurs at the health care consumer and provider interaction level through the assessment process, the provider conclusions, and the communication of findings. These professional activities are usually one-to-one interactions and are the direct care components of the health care services which form the basis for current services charges. However, documentation on the medical record and care coordination to implement the plan of care are just as important for quality of care. These indirect care components occur behind the scenes and adequate time is often not allocated. It seems logical that more control over the quality of care should occur at the clinical level whether a direct or indirect component of health care services. The professional nurses can provide invaluable input to quality of care discussions from their level of expertise as well as understanding of the perspectives of the health care consumer. The Patient-Centered Medical Home will help re-focus elements of quality control back to the clinical level.

Thus, the design for DIRECTED CARE is a team-based clinical service that includes the health care consumer as an active participant and is:

- Proactive/preventive
- Planned/systematic
- Comprehensive/integrated

The Design Elements

In DIRECTED CARE, health (wellness) care activities are compartmentalized from disease (illness) care activities, with acute and chronic care activities remaining the role and responsibility of medical care providers. Professional nurses become the primary orchestra leaders for health (wellness) care in collaboration with other team-based members. Providers of both illness and wellness care should see their roles as coaches (to reinforce and encourage change) for optimal wellness. The goal in compartmentalization is to clarify roles and responsibilities for independent professional nurse activities. There will always be gray areas between responsibilities for illness and wellness care. For example, professional nurses in DIRECTED CARE may coordinate illness care activities but not provide illness care. Consequently, good lines of communication between all parties are paramount for successful outcomes. Collaboration between the health care consumers and all providers should always be present, whether they are dealing with an illness or wellness issue.

A key element missing for the role of professional nurses in DIRECTED CARE is a clear method for documenting the time element and content of their independent activities for workload analysis and for billing services provided. Taken in the context that *professional* means knowledgeable and accountable, it becomes compelling to develop a separate unit of service to delineate professional nurses' independent functions. Professional nurses need to be identified as providers of services separate from but congruent with medical care services.

DIRECTED CARE is essentially be a hybrid care management model with activities related to organizing data, influencing health behavior, proposing evidence-based strategy options for wellness, and referring health care consumers to other health team members as appropriate. Collaborated referrals to case management, dieticians, behavioral health specialists, social workers, and clinical pharmacists should be included as independent professional nurse actions. Nursing diagnoses should also be included on the health/medical record Problem List if an International Classification of Diseases, Revision 9 (ICD-9) code or upcoming ICD-10 code is not available. International codes should take precedence over nursing diagnoses as long as they communicate the same condition. Nursing diagnosis entries would be with the understanding that professional nurses are addressing issues that are long-standing problems and have a written action plan with specific goals in collaboration with the health care consumer. Examples could be a coping problem, impairment with vision, hearing, mobility or dexterity, or a sleeping problem. Conferring with the medical care provider is essential to have a collaborative action plan for similar health or medical issues.

Consolidation and simplicity are major themes throughout the DIRECTED CARE process. Planned visits with coordinated pre-visit activities will be established for specific preventive and chronic care needs. A medical plan of care for each chronic condition will be incorporated into a consumer's health monitoring plan. Utilization will be reviewed to compare plans of care to actual services/interventions provided. Activities of professional nurses in DIRECTED CARE will encompass more cognitive skills for leadership and management than technical, procedural skills.

In summary, the desired overall goals of DIRECTED CARE are to: (1) guide health care consumers to optimal wellness; (2) provide order to the flow of information in a complex, multidimensional health care system; (3) analyze individual health care consumer utilization patterns; and (4) develop accountable units of service for independent professional nurse activities in ambulatory primary care.

Goal 1. Guide Health Care Consumers to Optimal Wellness.

Conduct annual Wellness Checks

Having an annual Wellness Check will facilitate keeping health care consumers on track to an optimal level of wellness. Annual visits could also eliminate the facility-imposed requirements for routine screening questions based on interpretation of JCAHO standards whether or not they have relevance to the visit or encounter, e.g., questions about depression and smoking. The Wellness Check should have dedicated time for face-to-face interaction after maximizing pre-visit coordination via telephone or e-mail with other clerical staff as appropriate. It is perceived that the design for planned visits will be used to set up preventive care or Wellness Check visits. Recommended preventive care measures, including screening tests specific to age and gender, should be arranged prior to the Wellness Check so that results will be available at the time of the visit. Pregnancy is considered a special circumstance that would be monitored outside the annual process. Well Baby and Well Child visits also fit outside the annual time frame until age three.

Wellness Checks are centered on recommendations from the U.S. Preventive Service Task Force (USPSTF). Important sources for age and gender preventive care recommendations are: (1) the U.S. Preventive Service Task Force's *Guide for Clinical Preventive Services*[30] and (2) the Electronic Preventive Services Selector (ePSS),[31] available as an electronic web-based tool or as a PDA. The minimum initial and annual adult physical assessment should be B/P, weight and height with BMI calculation, plus functional areas – mobility, dexterity, cognitive abilities, vision, and hearing. A comprehensive health history should be a com-ponent of the initial Wellness Check to serve as a pivotal contribution to a completed baseline. Annual updates should include medical events since the last Wellness Check, current personal health behaviors, chang-es in family history, work history, home environment, and a 24-hour food/beverage recall questionnaire to review the health care consumer's customary food choices. The American Academy of Pediatrics outlines details for children in *Bright Futures: Guidelines for Health Supervision of Infants, Children and Adolescents.*[32] Health monitoring activities for children's growth and development for all age groups is specified in the *Bright Futures* reference, including talking points for anticipatory guidance. It is important to inquire about health concerns prior to the actual assessment and then review during the interaction with the health care consumer to validate that those concerns were addressed.

A nurse practitioner will conduct a targeted health maintenance ex-amination (HME), warranted by functional deficits and USPSTF recommendations for age and gender. Additional time allotted for adolescents with the nurse practitioner will allow a discussion period for personal health behaviors, especially safe sex, food choices and substance use, and psychosocial issues often present during the teenage years. Adolescents are expected to assume more responsibility for their person-al health as they advance in age. More one-on-one time with a health care professional will provide teenagers the opportunity to establish growth as decision makers for their own health issues and obtain a better understanding of health risk management.

It is expected that immunization status will be assessed and recom-mendations made in accordance with the Advisory Committee for Immunizations Practices (ACIP). Immunizations can be administered by technical staff members with that explicit skill. A quiz type tool, "What Vaccines do YOU Need?" is available to assess adolescent and adult immunization status.[33]

At some point during the adult Wellness Check, it would be benefi-cial for the health care consumer to enter current responses on some type of Wellness Checklist to reinforce awareness of healthy behaviors. A proposed example of an Adult Wellness Checklist is displayed in

Appendix F. Health care consumers would be instructed to enter their initials in the areas of positive behaviors. This type of questionnaire/checklist would need to be scanned into an electronic medical record. With all the technology advances, a form such as this could be available as a touch screen document for health care consumers to enter their current responses on each year.

The Wellness Check should be concluded with a discussion of findings, using motivational interviewing skills, to ascertain what health care consumers desire to do with the information. The section on the Health Monitoring Plan will present the way the desired course of action will be integrated into a collaborative plan of care. Anticipatory guidance as well as on-going DIRECTED CARE support for personal behavioral change or self-management skill development is addressed under the sections for consulting/advising and counseling/coaching.

The Affordable Care Act makes provisions for an annual Wellness Check for Medicare consumers. Reimbursement requires that certain elements for the Medicare Annual Wellness Visit be included and are outlined in Appendix G. When reviewing these elements for coordination of care, consideration should be given to what the health care consumer would receive in reference to a preventive care visit and consolidate when feasible. Medicare does not currently accept CPT codes for comprehensive preventive evaluation and management (E&M) but does accept certain specific procedure CPT codes under Medicare Part B Preventive Services. These coding requirements present an example of the administrative burden placed on the clinical personnel to coordinate care for the health care consumer and to insure payment for services based on the way the encounter is coded.

Multiple examples of matrix templates that outline recommended preventive care services for each age group and gender are available on the Internet from various sources. A key point to remember is that any preventive care matrix needs to be current. Use of templates and checklists also has a down side in that so much time and attention is devoted to filling out the spaces or boxes that the purpose may become overshadowed.

Health care consumers who need to schedule a chronic care follow-up the same month as the Wellness Check could have some activities done concurrently. Caution may be warranted for health care providers and consumers not to displace the importance of preventive care. It would be easy to slip back to a focus on illness. Time should be set aside for health care consumers to discuss their concerns for both wellness and chronic care issues. Referrals should be made to other health care professionals and community-based programs or services as indicated.

Creative ways to vary the Wellness Check each year are unlimited and will help both health care consumers and providers maintain interest in the process. At the beginning of each year, professional nurses can select an annual theme for promoting some aspect of health. e.g., "Eye Health – A Good Investment" or "Herbal and Supplement Precautions." Personal health behaviors can be assessed from a different approach and feedback illustrated on a scorecard or graphic of a signal light with red meaning stop, serious consequences ahead; yellow meaning needs attention; and green meaning keep going. A particular health promotion issue could be selected as a talking point and reinforced with a printed handout to take home for reference. Appendix H offers an example for focusing on an environmental sensitivity subject. The possibilities are endless. Printed material presented in this manner is for review, to reinforce a particular point, or to provide specific details of information already discussed.

Identify biological, environmental, and behavioral health risks

There are three reasons to place emphasis on identifying risk factors. The first reason is that risk factors for disease are in the preclinical phase or are asymptomatic. Secondly, they are likely to affect more than one disease category or injury consequence. The third reason is risk factors provide the basis for designing a tailored health maintenance plan for each individual health care consumer.[34] These risk factors can be identified by gathering information about personal health behaviors, family history, home and work environment, physical examination, and specific testing. Most diseases are caused by several health risk factors, and generally health risk factors may contribute to more than one disease.

Health risks are defined as an exposure to possible loss, injury, or the probability of occurrence of a particular event.[35] Assessing risk factors includes appraisal of the characteristics, circumstances, or conditions that increase the probability of experiencing a particular event. Examples of risks factors are:

1. *Biological (uncontrollable)* – age, gender, genetics, adverse drug reaction
2. *Environmental (social and physical)* – exposure to chemicals; physical hazards that create unsafe areas; exposure to communicable disease; excessive noise; inadequate food, clothing, or shelter; hot or cold environment
3. *Behavioral* – unhealthy food choices, tobacco use, lack of physical activity, inadequate coping skills, substance use, inadequate sleep/rest

The health history will help identify past association with communicable diseases, both from history of having the disease and vaccines administered to prevent. Based on this information, the risk of a specific disease can be assessed. The health history will also assist to identify risk of disease from the family history. Genetic counseling referrals may be warranted in specific cases.

Environmental health involves the home, work setting, and community. The Centers for Disease Control and Prevention (CDC) provide annual reports of unintentional injuries. To prevent these unintentional injuries, a home safety survey should be encouraged on a periodic basis to help identify risks within the home environment. Safe habits at home minimize the risk of becoming a statistic. For instance, accidents with children's unsupervised handling of firearms could be prevented with proper storage of firearms to restrict access and with training for proper handling.

Knowing the occupational and community health risks is helpful in assessing health risk factors for the whole person concept even though these specific risks are generally managed outside primary care. The employer has legal responsibility for occupational health risks, but work-setting risks can be included in a comprehensive assessment of factors that place an individual at risk. Community health issues are addressed by the local public health agency. In addition to communicable diseases and biological hazards, air, water, and noise health issues are areas of concern for individuals residing in the community. Environmental risks for a specific geographical area can be identified by connecting to the "Explore Your Place History"[36] website and enter zip codes to identify chemicals within that area. Additional information about a specific chemical is available from the Agency for Toxic Substances & Disease Registry. Contact with the local public health agency or specific occupational setting may be necessary to ascertain information about a given health risk.

Personal health behaviors make an enormous impact on future health. The highest percentage of chronic conditions in the United States can be attributed to the personal health behaviors of individuals, as noted previously. It is estimated that personal health behaviors account for 50 percent of an individual's health status.[37] As far back as 1978, John Farquhar, MD, wrote a book entitled, *The American Way of Life Need Not Be Hazardous to Your Health*.[38] Despite two editions of the book to create movement toward change, the same basic American lifestyle lives on. The only notable change is that the word "lifestyle" has been replaced with the phrase "personal health behaviors." Thus, a need is created for awareness and modification in the way Americans live, and this assessment and counseling becomes an important part of preventive care for each health care consumer.

It would be beneficial for professional nurses to design a plan in collaboration with the health care consumer to prevent or minimize health risks. Identification of existing and/or potential health risks is the first step in risk management. Working with health care consumers to minimize risk factors over which they have a measure of control, such as personal health behaviors and environmental safety, will decrease their need for medical care. Woolf et al. lists interactive steps to take with health care consumers to establish awareness of their health risks and recommendations to modify controllable risk factors:

1. Identify health risks from subjective and objective data obtained.
2. Discuss which health risk factors can be controlled.
3. Inform of the downstream consequences of high health risks.
4. Discuss how controllable health risk factors can be modified.[39]

Following a health risk assessment for personal health behavior issues, health care providers should offer consumers sufficient information about the relationship between health risk and behavior to encourage change and suggest strategies for accomplishing behavioral change. The feelings and attitudes of the health care consumer about the health risk need the full attention and respect of the health care provider. The recommended strategies for changing behavior will be more relevant and have a greater likelihood of achieving results if placed in the framework of the health care consumer's living conditions.[40] Coaching and supporting activities will most likely be needed during follow-up and are discussed in more detail in that specific section that follows.

Health risk appraisal forms have been used in the past and are now available as interactive programs on the Internet. Unless the information is connected to the health care provider as an assessment tool, it becomes isolated and contributes to the fragmentation of health care information. In addition, these select health risk appraisal forms may not cover all three categories of health risk.

What greater asset for personal investment can individuals have than their health? Part of the rationale for annual Wellness Checks is to help keep health care consumers on track toward "getting healthy and staying healthy." It starts with evaluating health behavior and other health risk factors affecting the chance of developing a serious disease or experiencing a serious injury and continues with information sharing and coaching to an optimal level of health for a given individual.

Offer readily available professional nursing consultation

An important component of DIRECTED CARE is the development of an informed, confident health care consumer pointed toward optimal wellness and cost containment through effective utilization of health care services. Developing a health care consumer to this level requires a relationship process that evolves over time rather than resulting from a single intervention or program. Health care consumers are included in the decision making and learning approaches to self-management skills so that they adapt more effective choices to meet their individual circumstances. Health care team members must be willing to respect a health care consumer's right to choose even though the team members may not agree with the consumer's choice. Factors such as values, beliefs, attitudes, current life stresses, religion, previous experiences with the health care system, and life goals all influence health care consumer decision making. Understanding how these factors affect a given individual will increase the likelihood of success in personal goal attainment for a health care consumer.

Taking personal responsibility for maintaining one's health is dependent on the health care consumer's level of acceptance as an individual or parent/guardian. There may be issues with lack of confidence or dependence on others. Professional nurses have the opportunity to step in and assure that health care consumers have sufficient support and information to be the key decision maker in self-management of their health and to promote growth in their abilities and confidence. DIRECTED CARE is designed toward this endeavor.

When is professional nurse consultation needed? Situations requiring consultation can swing from acute to chronic health issues and from a health care consumer request regarding a problem to professional guidance following an assessment. Time and information available may dictate how the interaction is managed. Approaches to information sharing for counseling or consultation will become more complex with the transition from one-way telling to a more comprehensive interaction to find a fit with the individual or child's daily life. It can also be a professional challenge to recognize where the health care consumer is at any given point and direct movement to a healthier status. Adequate time allocation for this type of encounter with health care consumers is most likely not currently available in organizations, and adjustments would be required.

The advantage of the Patient-Centered Medical Home is that a relationship can be developed over time with better understanding of the health care consumer's perceptions, values, and beliefs. The role of the professional nurse is to offer information, guidance, and support. Guiding health care consumers to increase their abilities for choosing the right strategy at the right time helps them gain a sense of control that minimizes the effects of stress related to making the decision. Both preventive and chronic care encounters will present opportunities to influence change for controllable health risks.

The consulting expertise of the professional nurse is often used for triaging health-related problems. Telephone triage lines have been established by health care organizations and health care insurance plans for health care consumers to have immediate access for nurse consultation. The role may be labeled "advice nurse" or "nurse consultant." Professional nurses ascertain the acuity of a symptom from information presented and determine proper disposition from written medical protocols. Face-to-face triage may also occur in a urgent care setting. It is essential to have the guidance provided during the triage activity to be communicated to the health care provider managing the individual's illness care for follow-up. The advantage of having 24/7 nurse consultants for triaging health-related problems within the health care organization is access to the health care consumer's existing medical record.

The locus of control in managing health on a daily basis lies with the health care consumer. They are essentially their own personal care managers and make choices about their health behaviors 24/7. Health care providers have a professional responsibility to ensure individual consumer decisions are based on complete and accurate health care information. Health care consumers should not be left with an impression that they are being coerced toward a specific course of action. Building a relationship over time allows the health care team members a better understanding of the perception, values, and beliefs that influence the health care consumer's behavior.

Connecting the relevance of the information to the existing need maintains health care consumer interest in learning. *Tailoring* is the term used in communication theory to address relevance. Communication theory promotes tailoring messages as a means to motivate behavior change by matching content of messages to the health care consumer information needs and interests by framing the context meaningfully to the individual.[41] The Stages of Change Model[42] presents the impression that different messages are needed in the different stage of readiness. A tailored message requires assessing the health care consumer to create the appropriate content. Time needs to be allocated in each Wellness Check and chronic care visit to allow discussion of health care consumers' concerns and health issues in their daily lives.

Many utilization problems can be linked to health care consumers not knowing how to navigate the system effectively (getting desired outcome) and efficiently (timely with least number of resources). Health care consumers need to have an understanding of were they fit into the health care delivery system—how, when, and where to seek services. The lack of knowledge to address these issues beforehand will most likely result in a reactionary response increasing the sense of urgency. The situation is then perceived as an emergent need for medical intervention regardless of circumstances. Guiding health care consumers through the health care system efficiently can be best accomplished by orienting them to role expectations.

1. What is the Patient-Centered Medical Home (PCMH)?
2. How does DIRECTED CARE work?
3. What is their role as a health care consumer?
4. How do they manage acute episodes resulting from injury or disease?

An explanation of what an emergent condition is and what a health care consumer should do if an emergency occurs is proactive planning. Emergency services are often utilized for non-urgent care. On the flip side, a health care consumer may delay treatment, not understanding the urgency. Knowing which conditions should not have treatment delayed and having contingency plans (where to go, how to get there, what to take) should decrease the stress level when an emergency occurs. Table 3.3 below outlines responsibilities for the health care consumer and provider to enable an individual to "get healthy and stay healthy."

Table 3.3.   Health Care Responsibilities

Type of Health Care	Individual Actions	Health Care Provider Actions
Preventive Care	• Maintain weight BMI < 27. • Make healthy food choices. • Eat a variety of foods. • Limit salt. • Avoid fried foods. • Do moderate intensity activity 30 minutes daily. • Get adequate sleep. • Manage stress. • Avoid addictive substances-drugs, alcohol, tobacco. • Practice safe sex. • Maintain safe environment and/or safety practices. • Schedule health maintenance exams appropriate for age group. • Seek education or counseling for health problem as necessary.	• Promote healthy personal behaviors and wellness. • Perform health maintenance exams. • Provide consultation when requested or medically indicated. • Offer health coaching and support as needed.
Acute Care	• Initiate self-care for early intervention. • Seek medical assistance when needed.	• Conduct medical evaluations as needed. • Consult/counsel for self-care information. • Coach/support self-care skills.
Chronic Care (Illness > 3 months)	• Conduct self-management and seek assistance as needed. • See Health Care Provider as requested for follow-up visits.	• Perform medical surveillance. • Conduct clinical interventions to improve condition and minimize complications. • Provide consultation and counseling as indicated.

The difference between consulting and counseling may not be clear. For purposes of this discussion, *consultation* or *advising* will include stating professional opinions, impressions, or recommendations. Additionally, setting priorities or relaying evidence-based facts will be considered a consultation. Interactions with health care consumers will usually be episodic. *Counseling* or *coaching* will involve discussions to incorporate health care consumer actions into their daily lives – whether to initiate or modify a medical plan of care, to develop self-management skills, or to change personal behaviors, will be considered – and basically will occur during multiple encounters.

Counsel/Coach behavioral change and self-management skill development

Self-management has been stated as an important component to modify utilization patterns of health care consumers. The first step is to evaluate a health care consumer's ability (knowledge and skill) and willingness (confidence) to perform a given task. External barriers, such as lack of resources or social support within the environment, can also cause interference with a health care consumer's willingness or ability to take action. The professional nurse should facilitate minimizing or eliminating the internal (low skill and confidence) and external barriers.

Professional nurses will provide the leadership appropriate to develop decision making and behavior change of health care consumers for their own or their children's everyday lives. Family or household member involvement should be encouraged in the self-management process to help support the 24/7 picture in the home environment. Coaching will help health care consumers understand their weaknesses and find their strengths to fit self-management into their own or their children's lives. The goal is to assist in organizing their care so it has minimal impact on their daily activities. As children grow and develop, the dynamics between health care providers, and their parent(s)/guardian will change. Children are expected to become more involved in decision making for managing their own lives.

The Situational Leadership Model[43] can provide a structure for determining what leadership style would be warranted based on the health care consumer's ability and willingness to accomplish a specific task. Facilitating development of self-management and decision making skills will allow the health care consumer to become more independent.

The Situational Leadership Model, which was mainly written for employee interactions, has been blended with self-efficacy theory[44] to assist professional nurses in assessing the level at which health care consumers are making decisions about their health care. This level is described as the ability (knowledge and skill) and commitment (confidence and motivation) of individuals to take responsibility for directing their own behavior. The term used to identify the highest level of ability and commitment has been changed from "delegating" to "empowering." The goal of situational leadership can be to "help individuals understand and share expectations in their environment so they can gradually learn to supervise their own behavior and become responsible, self-motivated individuals"[45] or "to provide an environment that permits an individual to move along the development continuum."[46] Both statements provide a perspective for the application of situational leadership by professional nurses to influence health care consumers' changes in personal health behaviors.

In DIRECTED CARE, the professional nurse analyzes the situation and then guides/supports health care consumers according to their identified abilities and commitment levels. Different leadership styles are used depending on the situation.

Health Care Consumer Start Point	Leadership Approach
Low ability/low commitment	Directing
Low ability/high commitment	Coaching
High ability/high commitment	Supporting
High ability/high commitment	Empowering

Additional information and a graphic presentation about situational leadership for the application by professional nurses to influence behavioral change are depicted in Table 3.4.

Table 3.4. Leadership Action Grid to Influence Behavior

High		S3 **Supporting** *High Ability* *Low Confidence*	S2 **Coaching** *Low Ability* *High Confidence*	
	S4 **Empowering** *High Ability* *High Confidence*			S1 **Directing** *Low Ability* *Low Confidence*
Low				

Relationship / Supportive Actions (vertical axis, Low → High)

Low ← → High
Directive Actions
Task or Behavior

Able and Willing	Able and Unwilling	Unable but Willing	Unable and Unwilling

High ← → Low
Readiness

Leadership - inspiring other to make a change

Supportive Actions - extent to which health care provider engages in multi-way communication. This includes listening, encouraging, facilitating, clarifying, and giving social or emotional support. Focus is developing motivation.

Directive Actions - extent to which health care provider engages in spelling out the tasks and responsibilities of the health care consumer. This includes telling individuals what to do, how to do it, when to do it, and where to do it, as well as who's to do it. Focus is developing competence.

Readiness - the ability (knowledge and skill) and willingness (confidence and commitment) of individuals to take responsibility for directing their own behavior.

Adapted from:

Ken Blanchard, John P. Carlos, and Alan Randolph. *The 3 Keys to Empowerment.* (San Francisco, CA: Berrett-Koehler Publishing, 2001), 23.

Albert Bandura, Self-Efficacy: *The Exercise of Control.* (New York, NY: W. H. Freeman, 1997).

A given situation may necessitate clear, precise directions be given to accomplish a specific task within a sensitive time frame. The goal is to increase the health care consumer's confidence and ability in doing the task. More detail of interactions with each leadership approach is presented in Appendix I.

Recognizing the need for changing personal health habits and coaching for that change can be compared to the activity of gardening as presented in Table 3.5 below.

Table 3.5. Personal Behavior Change Compared to Gardening

Gardening Activity	Professional Nurse Activity
Determine appropriate planting selections for geographical region	Gather data – complete history taking and screening Tests
Prepare soil	Assess – identify problem(s)
Determine what to plant	Inform what risks are present and future impact or Consequences
Lay out planting plan for rows	Determine readiness; establish goals
Plant seed according to depth and spacing recommendations	Discuss perceptions and barriers
Water	Coach/support; influence; motivate
Weed	Adjust plan or strategies as needed
Harvest Positive yield – enjoy	Provide affirmations for change in physical parameters and/or health risks; praise accomplishment no matter how small
Low yield; no yield – analyze contributing conditions; factor in for next crop	Identify the barriers or conditions interfering with progress to change; collaborate and restructure plan or coaching strategies;

Growth (change) happens over time and is optimized with periodic watering and weeding. This emphasizes the importance of a continued time-related relationship with health care consumers. Their growth is seen as understanding how changing their behavior will improve their health and movement in a desired direction.

Guiding individuals down certain paths is a relational process in which trust and confidence are built over time. Health care consumers can gain insight from professional nurses on how to fit aspects of their medical plan of care or behavioral change into their lives and find a new way of living. A successful endeavor may require interaction with more than one professional team members and with reinforcement along the way.

Influencing change for unhealthy personal behaviors is the most effective means to promote health. However, it cannot succeed if the health care consumer lacks motivation or support. Individuals often see unhealthy behavior as enjoyable or deeply rooted in their lifestyle or culture.[47] The intent of DIRECTED CARE is to establish a nurturing professional nurse role to develop health care consumers' abilities to independently solve problems in their daily health management. Motivational interviewing is used to ascertain perspective of problems from the viewpoint of the health care consumer. Referral to Behavioral Health for cognitive behavior therapy can be considered to assist with changing the way behavior is perceived.

Goal 2. Provide Order to the Flow of Information in a Complex, Multidimensional Health Care System.

Inject planned visits for preventive and chronic care

Planned visits for chronic disease are congruent with the Planned Care Model. The purpose of planned visits is to have information available at the time of the visit to evaluate the disease status and to focus attention on one health issue. This devoted time allows the health care consumer and providers collectively to compare the status of management goals, to express concerns and problems encountered, and to strengthen self-management skills. Planned visits can be set up as one-on-one or group visits with the understanding that time is allocated to discuss the health care consumer's personal concerns and any modification to the medical plan of care. Pre-visit activities are accomplished to maximize the face-to-face time during the planned visit.

Health care consumers become aware that the time is dedicated to a discussion of their chronic condition only, and they are expected to be an active participant in the discussion. The case for planned visits as a venue for improving chronic care is summed up: "Too often, caring for chronic illness features an uninformed passive patient, interacting with an unprepared practice team, resulting in frustrating, inadequate encounters."[48]

Aside from chronic care, a planned visit for preventive care should be bundled as part of the annual Wellness Check. Having designated time set aside for preventive care places an element of importance on the activity both for the health care consumer and provider. Well Baby and Well Child visits are already established as planned visits whereby the parent/guardian has an understanding up front of the purpose of the scheduled interaction with a health professional.

Create an organized, comprehensive Summary Health Care Record

Most health care practice settings do not have a standardized or organized approach to collecting, summarizing, or reviewing individual data, although having one would facilitate workflow. A method of presenting health data is needed that: (1) facilitates the flow of information for rapid review; (2) enhances the communication of health care services received to minimize duplication; and (3) decreases the need for health care consumers to repeat various aspects of their current and past medical histories.

The health/medical record is an important part of communicating a health care consumer's status and the care received within the health care system. There is no universal order for hard-copy or electronic medical records, even though the traditional SOAP (Subjective, Objective, Assessment, and Plan) format can be extracted from review of documentation of a visit. As Michael Stelman, MD describes: records are overflowing with information to include problem lists, medication lists, various flow sheets (e.g. disease-oriented parameters, specific laboratory data, preventive care parameters), immunization lists, and previous histories and physicals. Health care providers must review multiple pages to find out what the health care consumer needs. Then they must take the chronologically listed, but unrelated, information, mentally re-order it by disease or organ system, gather today's data, and finally integrate the data to develop an appropriate treatment plan.[49]

An organized, comprehensive summary will facilitate efficient use of the health care provider's time minimizing the effort required to find and assimilate information.

Variables linked to the degree of difficulty for data consolidation and organization are:

1. Existing location of data – inside or outside of organization
2. Number of records required
3. Organization and clarity of data
4. Health care consumer participation in assembling data

The Microsoft Access program has the potential for development of a comprehensive health summary. The Chronic Disease Electronic Management System (CDEMS)[50] used this format for its public domain software program to manage chronic disease. A discussion of CDEMS as a flexible software program is presented in Appendix J. Why not look closely at Microsoft Access for organizing a potential comprehensive Summary Health Care Record with its successful application by CDEMS? Many primary care clinics have Microsoft Office already. However, an existing organization's Electronic Medical Record (EMR), such as AHLTA (Armed Forces Health Longitudinal Technology Application), could possibly be modified for data to be ordered by system in the same manner as the proposed system.

The proposed system should have sections for (1) Medical Conditions/Health Risks, (2) Services/Interventions, and (3) Pharmaceutical Agents. The data would be ordered by system to minimize synthesis of information when reviewing and would be placed into a consistent format such as:

S00	General	S07	Musculosketal
S01	Skin	S08	Neurological
S02	HEENT	S09	Mental Health/Psychiatric
S03	Respiratory	S10	Endocrine
S04	Cardiovascular	S11	Hematologic/Lymphatic
S05	Gastrointestinal	S12	Allergic/Immunologic
S06	Genitourinary		

Data entry should be facilitated by use of drop-down lists, look-up tables, and a computer touch screen. A brief example of a look-up table for one system (S01 Skin) is displayed in Appendix K. Entry categories for the Summary Health Care Record are presented in Appendix L. A column designed to enter "Current" or "Past" would allow reporting out either or both. As examples, a report listing all current medical conditions, recent interventions, and current medications could be accessed by designating to report the "Current," listings or a report could be generated to list all entries for a given system. The organization will make the determination of which entries would receive the "Past" designation (e.g., all resolved medical conditions, services/interventions greater than 3 years ago, medications no longer taken). Keeping all immunizations in the "Current" category would provide a record of immunization status.

The Summary Health Care Record must be in some consistent format to enable transfer of information to multiple settings and rapid review of the contents. It will be imperative to have safeguards in place to maintain confidentially and a way to block reporting sensitive information when desired. Updates for a comprehensive summary of an individual's health and medical data must be routinely scheduled to keep the information accurate and meaningful. A current copy of the Summary Health Care Record could also accompany a referral or transfer of care records. However, copies should be released with health care consumer consent in accordance with the Health Insurance Portability and Accountability Act (HIPAA) regulations.

A printed copy of the Summary Care Record should be given to the health care consumer to serve as a possible Personal Health Record along with encouragement to keep the copy readily available in the event an Emergency Room visit becomes necessary. It is highly conceivable that this form will be the most updated Personal Health Record in the health care consumer's possession. It is logical to attempt to maintain one's own Personal Health Records, but in reality it often gets put off for other pressing matters.

DIRECTED CARE should serve as shared information custodian in partnership with the health care consumer. A health care consumer's own or child's copy could serve as a working copy by allowing extra space on the Summary Health Care Record to note additional conditions, services, interventions, or medications. The health care consumer could also line through medications no longer taken or note changes in existing medications. The working copy would then be presented at the Check-in Visit to assist with updating the Summary Health Care Record or would serve as a current record of health issues anytime in the interim when episodic or chronic care is needed.

In general, a Summary Health Care Record could also be used for a Emergency Medical Data Card and/or a Personal Health Record as previously mentioned. What an efficient use of health data – a single record for personal health record, an emergency data base, an on-going medical history, recorded parameters for chronic disease management, and tracking mechanism for tracking preventive care interventions, all on a single form! England has a Summary Care Record (SCR)[51] along these lines. Therefore, the optimal Summary Health Care Record would be one in a universal format.

Effectiveness of a computer-generated Summary Health Care Record will be enhanced by engaging the health care providers in the design and implementation. "New technologies will fail or prove inefficient unless its users feel comfortable with it. Post installation training alone won't turn people into ardent users of a new system."[52] The literature has documentation of numerous project failures due to lack of end user engagement in the project from the beginning. Health care personnel need to see an Information Technology project as an enabler and integral part of their work.[53]

DIRECTED CARE activities start with a comprehensive approach towards consolidation and organization of health data. Professional nurses will work in collaboration with health care team members and the health care consumer to provide an integrated health care record. If coded correctly, this summary of health and medical information could be used for reports in lieu of additional data entries on separate software programs, such as population management.

The information printed on the following example of a Summary Health Care Record in Table 3.6 is for illustrative purposes only and may not be congruent with clinical guidelines.

Table 3.6.   Summary Health Care Record

Name: T. B. Goody   Age: 36   Birth Month: OCT   Date Completed: 10/31/11

ALERTS

◆ Communication Alert:
[•] None at present
[ ] English language barrier
  ( ) Speaks only_____
  ( ) Unable to read English
[ ] Limited formal education
[ ] Cognitive impairment (294.90)
[ ] Vision impairment (369.00)
[ ] Hearing impairment (389.90)
[ ] Speech impairment (784.5)

◆ Mobility Alert:
[•] None at present
[ ] Upper extremity impairment (V49.1)
[ ] Lower extremity impairment (V49.2)
[ ] Low activity tolerance

◆ Health Habits Alert:
[•] Healthy food choices
[•] Physical activity
[•] Sleep/Rest
[ ] Stress level
[ ] Tobacco use
[ ] Alcohol use
[ ] Environmental safety Issues

◆ Medical Decision Maker:
[•] Self
[ ] Parent/Guardian
[ ] Designated Party by Power of Attorney
[ ] Living Will

◆ Pharmacological Alerts
[ ] No known medication allergies
[•] Known medication allergies
[•] Known adverse medication reactions

◆ Other Allergy Alerts
[ ] Diagnostic Substances/Dyes_____
[ ] Latex
[ ] Adhesive
[•] Food <u>Seafood</u>_____
[ ] Insect _____
[ ] Other _____

MEDICAL CONDITIONS/HEALTH RISKS				
	ICD-9 Code	Name	Comments	C/P
S00	278.02	Obesity, BMI >30	Flow sheet available	C
S01	882.0	Hand Laceration	Use of sharp at home	C
S02	V15.9	Health Risk – Eye fatigue	Prolonged viewing computer monitor	C
	V15.9	Health Risk- Eye injury	Uses power equipment	C
	367.1	Myopia (Near-sighted)	Wears corrective lenses	C
S03				
S04	V17.4	+ Family History--hypertension	Paternal grandmother; father	C
S05				
S05				
S06	663.0	Delivery, cesarean	Full-term live infant	C
	V16.3	+ Family History--breast	Mother--dx @ age 48	C
S07				
S08				
S09	648.4	Depression, post-partum		C
S10	250.02	Diabetes Mellitus, Type 2 Uncontrolled	Managed by Secondary Provider	C
S11				
S12	052.9	Varicella (chicken pox)	Self-reported @ age 8	C
	V15.04	Allergic to Seafood	Risk for anaphylaxis	C
	V14.0	Allergic to PCN	Rash	C

SERVICES/INTERVENTIONS						
	Category	Name	Date	Comments/Findings	Location	C/P
S00	I04 Provider Encounter	Wellness Check	10/00/12	DUE		C
	I04 Provider Encounter	Wellness Check	10/31/11	Desires wt loss	First Primary Clinic	C
	I06 Specific Exam	Wt/BMI	10/31/11	180 lbs/BMI 31	First Primary Clinic	C
	I12 Counsel/Coach	Weight Reduction	10/31/11	BMI >30	First Primary Clinic	C
S01	I03 Surgery	Laceration Repair	05/27/12	Right hand	Urgent Care Clinic	C
S02						
S03						

	Category	Name	Date	Comments/Findings	Location	C/P
			SERVICES/INTERVENTIONS			
S04	I06 Specific Exam	B/P	10/31/11	122/76	First Primary Clinic	C
S05						
S06	I01 Hospitalization	Term Delivery	08/04/11	Live Birth	St Elizabeth Med Ctr, Jessup, WY	C
	I03 Surgery	C-Section	08/04/11	Prolapsed cord		C
	I04 Provider Encounter	Prenatal Care	12/15/11	Transferred to Dr. Wills	Jessup, WY	C
	I08 Lab Test	Pregnancy Test	12/05/11	Positive	First Primary Clinic	C
	I09 Diagnostic Imaging	Mammogram	10/31/11	Declined	First Primary Clinic	C
	I06 Specific Exam	Pelvic	10/31/11	No significant findings	First Primary Clinic	C
	I08 Lab Test	Pap Smear	10/31/11	No significant findings	First Primary Clinic	C
S07						
S08						
S09	I13 Referral	Behavioral Health	08/10/11	Post-partum Depression		C
	I04 Provider Encounter	Diabetes Planned Visit	08/00/12	DUE	Secondary Provider	C
S10	I08 Lab Test	HbA1c	08/00/12	DUE	Secondary Provider	C
	I08 Lab Test	HbA1c	02/00/12	DUE	Secondary Provider	C
	I06 Provider Encounter	Diabetes Planned Visit	07/18/11		Secondary Provider	
	I08 Lab Test	HbA1c	07/18/11	8.0	Secondary Provider	C
	I06 Provider Encounter	Diabetes Planned Visit	04/11/11		Secondary Provider	
	I08 Lab Test	HbA1c	04/11/11	8.2	Secondary Provider	C
S11						
S12	I10 Pharmaceutical	Td Vaccine	05/27/12	Laceration repair	Urgent Care Clinic	C
	I10 Pharmaceutical	Influenza vaccine	10/31/11			C

	Category	Name	Date	Action	Dose and Frequency	C/P
		PHARMACEUTICAL AGENTS				
S00	Supplement	Multiple Vitamins	OTC		1 daily	C
S01						
S02						
S03						
S04						
S05						
S06						
S07						
S08	Analgesic	Ibuprofen	OTC		200mg	C
S09	● Adverse Reaction	Sertraline HCL *Zoloft®* (insomnia)	09/27/11	STOP		C
S10	Anti-Diabetic Agent	Metformin *Glucophage®*			500mg bid	C
S11						
S12	▶ Allergic Reaction	PCN (rash)				C
	Anaphylactic Precaution	Epinephrine Pen (seafood ingestion)	10/31/11	START		C

Map out an integrated Health Monitoring Plan

Case management uses care mapping to chart pathways for designated benchmarks along the route to recovery or a stable condition. Why not transform this model to create a plan to monitor a consumer's health, integrating preventive care and chronic care recommendations for a designated time frame? Professional nurses in DIRECTED CARE will outline the Health Monitoring Plan for a health care consumer based on age and gender-specific preventive care integrated with the medical plan of care for all chronic conditions over a twelve-month period.

The medical plan of care for each chronic condition should be solicited from the medical provider managing the condition in sufficient time prior to a planning session to integrate the information. Requesting a written medical plan of care annually, one to two months prior to each birth month, may demonstrate the importance for care management. It projects out for a year to illustrate the way to manage a chronic illness during that time frame based on existing circumstances. A set request form is more likely to have information needed to be included on the Health Monitoring Plan. It is expected that a note to the health care provider to explain the specific need for the information and what the time frame is for returning the information will accompany the request. Health care providers working outside the organization will also need a signed authorization to release the medical information, and it should be included with the request for information. An example of a request form for a Medical Plan of Care is shown in Appendix M.

The Health Monitoring Plan form should reflect a collaborative effort to present a projected plan of care set for effective outcomes by integrating the perspectives of all providers and the health care consumer and should be updated annually. It consolidates information and projects health care needs into time frames and serves as a form similar to a planning calendar. Personal health goals are solidified for the upcoming year. A copy should be available for the Primary Care Manager to periodically review. The Health Monitoring Plan could also be a helpful document for planned chronic care visits. Table 3.7 below illustrates a sample Health Monitoring Plan.

Table 3.7. Health Monitoring Plan

Name: T. B. Goody   Age: 36   Birth Month: OCT   Date Completed: 10/31/11

INTERVALS					
	Monthly	Every 2 Months	Every 3 Months	Every 6 Months	Annual
October	•	•	•	•	•
November	•				
December	•	•			
January	•		•		
February	•	•			
March	•				
April	•	•	•	•	
May	•				
June	•	•			
July	•		•		
August	•	•			
September	•				
	↓	↓	↓	↓	↓
HEALTH MONITORING ACTIVITIES					
Assessments/Exams	Visual Foot Exam		Diabetes Check w/ Dr Fitzgibbon B/P	Dental Exam	Vision Exam and Retinal Exam **Wellness Check**
Labs	Daily Blood Glucose before meals and at bedtime		HbA1c		Lipid Profile Microalbumin Creatinine
Other					/nfluenza Vaccine (Oct-Mar)

COMMENTS
Request using your copy of Summary Health Care Record as worksheet for recording new information and lining out information that no longer applies.

Health Care Provider: (Signature)   Date:
Nurse Care Director: (Signature)   Date:

POSITIVE HEALTH ACTIONS

1 Increased skill to perform timely blood glucose testing. Discussed understanding of importance and purpose.
2 Kept food diary for one month and identified possible problem areas.
3 Exploring options for daily moderate physical activity
4 Immunizations are current.

HEALTH RISKS/UNHEALTHY PERSONAL BEHAVIOR RECOMMENDATIONS

1 Risk of diabetic complications minimized with improved blood glucose control and will decrease frequency of blood glucose monitoring and provider visits.
2 Weight loss likely to help with improved blood glucose control.
3 Prevent eye injury by wearing eye protection when operating power equipment.
4 High blood pressure is a health risk with family history and lipid panel results. Recommend watching salt and fat intake.
5 Suggest increasing amount of non-starchy vegetables in daily food choices.
6 Mother's history of breast cancer before menopause increases your health risk. Recommend close monitoring.
7 Scheduled break periods during computer use will lessen fatigue or vary work tasks.
8 Make family/friends aware of seafood allergy and where you keep EpiPen.

PERSONAL HEALTH GOALS FOR NEXT TWELVE MONTHS

1 Loose 1 pounds/week (eat ~500 calories less per day). Goal = 145 lbs
2 Watch food quantity by eating smaller portions.
3 Increase physical activity with 20-minute walk with dog each day.
4 Replace soda pop with filtered water.

ADMINISTRATIVE PREPARATION FOR UNEXPECTED MEDICAL EVENT

1 Medical Power of Attorney Completed [•] Yes   [ ] No   [ ] Not Desired
2 Advanced Directives Completed   [•] Yes   [ ] No   [ ] Not Desired
3 Medical Data Available for Emergency [ ] Yes   [•] No

(Signature)   **Date:**

Health care consumers should be actively involved in getting information from their secondary and tertiary providers, especially outside an organization where primary care is received. Nurses tend to gravitate toward doing care coordination *for* health care consumers whereas the focus should be doing the coordination *with* them and encouraging them to take more of the responsibility. DIRECTED CARE strives to assist health care consumers to take more responsibility for their care. At the end of creating the new Health Monitoring Plan, the health care consumer should be encouraged to provide a copy to their other providers. Care coordination is enhanced and care becomes more efficient when all involved are "on the same page" and when health care consumers are active participants.

Designing a twelve-month integrated plan, followed by a retrospective review of the services received, will allow the professional nurse to ascertain whether the health care consumer received the right service at the right level and at the right time. Problem areas can be identified and solutions collaboratively formulated to improve utilization patterns.

Goal 3. Analyze Individual Health Care Consumer Utilization Patterns

Conducting an annual review of utilization patterns provides an evaluation of how the previous year's health monitoring plan fared. It would be a chronological review of services and activities for an individual for the past twelve months. The purpose of this evaluation process would be to:

- Evaluate use of resources for necessity, efficiency, and appropriateness
- Determine consistency of utilization with Health Monitoring Plan
- Establish the need for coaching on better utilization patterns

The review of utilization differs in purpose from that driven by insurance payment authorization. Even though cost containment is a concern, the primary focus is to determine how services provided fit into the Health Monitoring Plan and how other acute care services correlated with the purpose of the encounter. The review process is expected to note areas for more effective or efficient utilization of health care resources for discussion with the consumer and can lead to the possible secondary benefit of cost-containment.

Prior to the annual Wellness Check, the evaluation of the health care consumer's utilization patterns for the past twelve months can be conducted. This would allow the opportunity to discuss findings with the health care consumer in conjunction with the planned visit. Information about utilization can be obtained from the accounting departments where health care consumers have obtained services over the past twelve months, from review of the medical record, and from the consumers themselves. The professional nurse should solicit information about the use of Complimentary and Alternative Medicine (CAM) services as well as herbal or supplement use to obtain a complete picture of all health care interventions utilized.

High utilization could be referred to case management in collaboration with a primary care manager and the health care consumer to allow an in-depth evaluation of options for utilization resources in a more cost-effective manner. In case management, specific time is dedicated for that purpose, and the search is conducted and analyzed by an experienced person.

Goal 4. Develop Accountable Units of Service for Independent Professional Nursing Activities in Ambulatory Primary Care

WANTED – a unit of service that reveals the independent DIRECTED CARE activities of professional nurses as providers.

How will units of service be used? There are three management applications – planning resource allocation, productivity determination, and billing services. The planning phase for using units of services is discussed in the section for allocation of professional nurses' time in Chapter 5. Independent professional nurse activities stand out and make a statement by having a billable unit of service with its description.

Ambulatory care services are currently listed as procedures provided and designated by CPT (Common Procedural Terminology) codes published by the American Medical Association. These codes are intended for physicians as providers but can be used by nurse practitioners and physician assistants. Few CPT codes are designated for non-physician services without physician supervision. The majority of the CPT codes are for face-to-face encounters with related time, such as coordination, built into the fee for that coded service. Indirect care (related but not face-to-face) is an important aspect for effective care but currently has reimbursement issues. There are relatively new CPT codes for telephone consultations with the health care consumer for use under limited circumstances. Taking into account that one of the PCMH joint principles is for enhanced access, additional or expanded CPT codes for telephone consultation, and maybe even e-mail, may soon be available.

The most common ambulatory primary care unit of service is clinic visits. Nursing activities have been support activities. "Nurse only" visits have been identified for blood pressure monitoring and health education. The time is at hand to argue the case that independent professional nursing service has value and should be reimbursed directly. Case management and care coordination by professional nurses have demonstrated value but have been often folded into support services. Elements of a workload currently qualified as *visit* or *telephone call* need to capture what occurs during the service interaction to manage resources. Coding should not become so finite that personnel time required to record the codes exceeds the benefit of having them.

There are five basic categories for independent professional nursing activities in DIRECTED CARE. These activities incorporate dimensions of professional nursing leadership and management expertise for interactions with health care consumers, their families, and PCMH team members:

- Evaluating/Assessing
- Conferring/Coordinating
- Consulting/Advising
- Counseling/Coaching
- Organizing/Sequencing

A unit of service that accounts for professional nurse workload transferable to productivity analysis and billable service is the target. It would be worthwhile to look outside the box and develop an accounting unit other than current practice for professional nursing services. For DIRECTED CARE activities, it is proposed that time increments be the unit of service, which translates into the perception that professional time is being purchased. This is the common billing practice for the legal profession. The health care service for DIRECTED CARE is professional nurse time. Units of service in time increments are flexible and can cover simple to complex, direct and/or indirect professional nurse activities. Time increments can be standardized. The unit of service for DIRECTED CARE is a 10-minute increment where 1 minute equals 0.1 unit of service. Fifteen minute increments have been used for workload determination or analysis, but this time increment limits flexibility. A five minute or 0.5 unit of service should be the minimum time increment allowed for calculating units of service as shown below.

Minutes	Unit of Service
5	0.5
10	1.0
15	1.5
20	2.0
25	2.5, etc.

Units of services fall under two categories:

1. *Consumer Direct Care Activities* – clinical time spent on activities providing services related to direct contact with consumer and/or family
   a. Evaluate/assess – data obtained about health care consumer or child through examination or interview and synthesized
   b. Confer/coordinate – communication with health care consumer and/or child to obtain or clarify information
   c. Consult/advise – interaction with health care consumer and/or child to provide information about a specific problem or issue
   d. Coach/support – interaction with health care consumer and/or child to motivate or influence actions; to guide toward improved health status or self-management

2. *Consumer Indirect Care Activities* – clinical time spent on activities providing services related to health care consumer and/or child but not done directly with consumer
   a. Evaluate/assess – data obtained about health care consumer or child; report review
   b. Plan/map – organize information, place in order, establish priories; write a report

c. Confer/coordinate – communication with other health care team members to discuss or refer individual health care consumer or child

d. Consult/advise – request or give opinion for further assessment of individual health care consumer or child with other health care team members

Why use units of service rather than just stating actual minutes for an activity? It allows for a block of time to be allocated rather than having to count every minute. Expected units of service can be established for re-occurring core activities, such as Wellness Checks for specific age and gender groups.

For continuity, nurse practitioners should continue to use medical service CPT codes for preventive care services – examinations, testing, immunizations. Health care services related to optimal wellness are in transition. It would be beneficial to document the time requirement and type of activity necessary to interact with health care consumers to capture time requirements for preventive care activities. CPT coding and recording units of service can be seen as a duplicated activity. Time should be allotted as non-productive time for an additional accounting measure. The amount of time professional nurses use in DIRECTED CARE activities should be part of the annual Utilization Review to capture the true picture of individual utilization of health care services over the previous twelve months.

Presenting billable time as units of service can serve the secondary purpose of illustrating to health care consumers the actual cost of the professional's time necessary to identify and solve the consumers' health problems. The knowledge of the cost of professional time can provide an incentive for the health care consumer to learn self-assessment skill or increase their participation in the process to decrease the need for professional time to coordinate care.

The Patient-Centered Medical Home model's emphasis on alternative accessibility (outside office visits) will broaden reimbursement opportunities. Tracking time for indirect care activities will help justify the need for reimbursement for activities required between visits. The door is open for policy makers to make additional changes in the way ambulatory care services are reimbursed. A special report from the

American Academy of Family Physicians perceives reimbursement reform being in an experimental or trial stage.[54] Medicare has piloted some new approaches to reimbursement. One model proposes the payment of a lump sum as a supplemental fee for service coordination to the health care provider. Could this same type of payment be considered for professional nurse activities in DIRECTED CARE? With on-going discussions to revamp reimbursement for the Patient-Centered Medical Home, an opportunity is afforded for professional nurses to create an avenue for reimbursement for DIRECTED CARE activities. Documenting units of service and constructing a unit cost will assist in justification of the time used by professional nurses for these activities. An article in *Family Practice Management*, written by Jeff Kullgren and Marcia Sibella, provides a discussion on six steps to unit cost analysis, or how much it costs to provide a service at the smallest practical unit (in this case, a unit of time).[55]

Notes

1. Institute for Healthcare Improvement. "Building an Effective Planned Care System for all Patients in Ambulatory Settings" in *Planned Care Guide*, 1, *http://www.ihi.org* (accessed June 20, 2012).

2. Institute for Healthcare Improvement. "Building an Effective Planned Care System for all Patients in Ambulatory Settings" in *Planned Care Guide*, 1, *http://www.ihi.org* (accessed June 20, 2012).

3. *Webster's New World College Dictionary*, 4th ed. (Cleveland, OH: Wiley, 2005), 407.

4. James F. Fries and others. "Beyond Health Promotion: Reducing Need and Demand for Medical Care," *Health Affairs* 17, no. 2 (1998): 77.

5. James F. Fries and others. "Beyond Health Promotion: Reducing Need and Demand for Medical Care." *Health Affairs* 17, no. 2 (1998): 74.

6. James F. Fries and others. "Beyond Health Promotion: Reducing Need and Demand for Medical Care." *Health Affairs* 17, no. 2 (1998): 74.

7. American Nurses Association. *Nursing Scope and Standards of Practice*, 2nd ed. (Silver Spring, MD: Nursebooks.org, 2010), 1.

8. National Organization of Nurse Practitioners Faculties (NONPF) and American Association of Colleges of Nursing (AACN). *Nurse Practitioner Primary Care Competencies in Specialty Areas: Adult, Family, Gerontological, Pediatric, and Women's Health* (Rockville, MD: U.S. Department of Health and Human Services, 2002).

9. World Health Organization. 6th Global Conference on Health Promotion (Geneva, Switzerland: The Bangkok Chapter for Health Promotion in a Global- ized World, August 11, 2005), *http://www.who.org.int/* (accessed June 27, 2012).

10. Institute of Medicine. *The Future of Nursing: Leading Change, Advancing Health (Summary)*, (Washington, DC: National Academy Press, 2010), S-3.

11. American Nurses Association. *Nursing Scope and Standards of Practice*, 2nd ed. (Silver Spring, MD: Nursebooks.org, 2010), 110.

12. Institute of Medicine. *The Future of Nursing: Leading Change, Advancing Health (Summary)*, (Washington, DC: National Academy Press, 2010), 2.

13. Centers for Disease Control and Prevention (CDC). "Chronic Diseases: The Power to Prevent; The Call to Control" National Center for Chronic Disease Prevention and Health Promotion (2009), 2, *http://www.cdc.gov/chronicdisease/resources/publications/AAG/pdf/chronic.pdf* (accessed July 3, 2012).

14. Steven H. Woolf, Steven Jonas, and Evonne Kaplan-Liss. *Health Promotion and Disease Prevention in Clinical Practice,* 2nd ed. (Philadelphia, PA: Lippincott Williams and Wilkins, 2008), xxxiv.

15. Hugh R. Leavell and E. Gurney Clark. *Preventive Medicine for the Doctor in His Community,* 2nd ed. (New York, NY: McGraw-Hill, 1965), 28.

16. James F. Fries and others. "Beyond Health Promotion: Reducing Need and Demand for Medical Care." *Health Affairs* 17, no. 2 (1998): 77.

17. Steven H. Woolf, Steven Jonas, and Evonne Kaplan-Liss. *Health Promotion and Disease Prevention in Clinical Practice,* 2nd ed. (Philadelphia, PA: Lippincott Williams and Wilkins, 2008), xxxviii.

18. Steven H. Woolf, Steven Jonas, and Evonne Kaplan-Liss. *Health Promotion and Disease Prevention in Clinical Practice,* 2nd ed. (Philadelphia, PA: Lippincott Williams and Wilkins, 2008), xxxviii.

19. Steven H. Woolf, Steven Jonas, and Evonne Kaplan-Liss. *Health Promotion and Disease Prevention in Clinical Practice,* 2nd ed. (Philadelphia, PA: Lippincott Williams and Wilkins, 2008), 129.

20. Richard L. Street, Jr. "Healing Communication: Clinician-Patient Communication," *Psychosocial Health Podcast* (June 13, 2011), para. 1, *http://www.healthpodcasts.blogspot.com/2011/06/healing-communication-clinican-patient.htm* (accessed June 20, 2012).

21. Richard L. Street, Jr. and others. "How Does Communication Heal? Pathways Linking Clinician-Patient Communication to Health Outcomes," *Patient Education and Counseling* 74 (2009): 299.

22. No Time to Teach Blog *Patient Education Means Information Sharing AND Coaching,* (March 28, 2011), 1, *http://www.notimetoteach.com/2011/twolevels/* (accessed February 10, 2012).

23. Steven H. Woolf, Steven Jonas, and Evonne Kaplan-Liss. *Health Promotion and Disease Prevention in Clinical Practice,* 2nd ed. (Philadelphia, PA: Lippincott Williams and Wilkins, 2008), 130.

24. McWhitney. "Forward 1: How to Motivate Healthy Behavior" in Rich Botelho, *Motivational Practice: Promoting Healthy Habits and Self-care of Chronic Disease* (Rochester, NY: MHH Publications, 2004), 3.

25. No Time to Teach Blog *Patient Education Means Information Sharing AND Coaching*, (March 28, 2011), 1, *http://www.notimetoteach.com/2011/twolevels/* (accessed February 10, 2012).

26. Nola J. Pender, Carolyn L. Murdaugh, and Mary Ann Parsons. *Health Promotion in Nursing Practice*, 6th ed. (Boston, MA: Pearson, 2011), 267-269.

27. Andrea I. Kabcenell, Jerry Langley, and Cindy Hupke. *Innovations in Planned Care. IHI Innovation Series White Papers.* (Cambridge, MA: Institute for Healthcare Improvement, 2006), 8-15.

28. Nola J. Pender, Carolyn L. Murdaugh, and Mary Ann Parsons. *Health Promotion in Nursing Practice*, 6th ed. (Boston, MA: Pearson, 2011), 38-46.

29. Ken Blanchard, John P. Carlos, and Alan Randolph. *The 3 Keys to Empowerment*, (San Francisco, CA: Berrett-Koehler Publishing, 2001), 22-23.

30. S. Department of Health and Human Services. *The Guide to Clinical Preventive Services 2010-2111*. Agency for Healthcare Research and Quality AHRQ Pub. No 10-0545 (2010), *http://www.USPreventiveTaskForce.org* (accessed July 18, 2012).

31. U.S. Department of Health and Human Services. *About ePSS. Electronic Preventive Services Selector.* Agency for Healthcare Research and Quality, *http://epss.ahrq.gov* (accessed February 12, 2012).

32. Joseph F. Hagan, Judith Shaw, and Paula M. Duncan. eds. *Bright Futures: Guidelines for Health Supervision of Infants, Children and Adolescents*, 3rd ed.(Elk Grove Village, IL: American Academy of Pediatrics 2008), *http://brightfutures.aap.org/pdfs/3rd-Edition-Guidelines-and-Pocket-Guide.html* (accessed July 18, 2012).

33. Centers for Disease Control and Prevention. "What Vaccines Do YOU Need?" *http://www2a.cdc.gov/nip/adultImmSched/* (accessed July 3, 2012).

34. Steven H. Woolf, Steven Jonas, and Evonne Kaplan-Liss. *Health Promotion and Disease Prevention in Clinical Practice,* 2nd ed. (Philadelphia, PA: Lippincott Williams and Wilkins, 2008), xii.

35. Ruth B. Murray, Judith P. Zentner, and Richard Yakimo. *Health Promotion Strategies Through the Life Span*, 8th ed. (Upper Saddle River, NJ: Prentice-Hall, 2008), 74.

36. "Explore Your Place History," ersi (February 22, 2011), *http//www.esri.com/industries/health/geomedicine/map.html* (accessed August 30,

37. National Business Group on Health. *Payment Systems, Government Policies and Market Incentives Should Refocus Efforts on Disease Prevention.* (Washington, DC, 2010), 2-3, *http://www.businessgrouphealth.org/pdfs/preventioncarepositionstatement.pdf* (accessed June 20, 2012).

38. John W. Farquhar. *The American Way of Life Need Not Be Hazardous to Your Health* (Reading, MA: Addison-Wesley Publishing, 1987).

39. Steven H. Woolf, Steven Jonas, and Evonne Kaplan-Liss. *Health Promotion and Disease Prevention in Clinical Practice,* 2nd ed. (Philadelphia, PA: Lippincott Williams and Wilkins, 2008), 10.

40. Steven H. Woolf, Steven Jonas, and Evonne Kaplan-Liss. *Health Promotion and Disease Prevention in Clinical Practice,* 2nd ed. (Philadelphia, PA: Lippincott Williams and Wilkins, 2008), xliii.

41. Barbara K. Rimer, and Matthew W. Kreuter. "Advancing Tailored Communication: A Persuasion and Message Effects Perspective," *Journal of Communication* 56, Supplement (2006): S188.

42. Gretchen L. Zimmerman, Cynthia G. Olsen, and Michael F. Bosworth. "A 'Stage of Change' Approach to Helping Patients Change Behavior," *American Family Physicians* 61, no.3 (2000): 1409-1416.

43. Ken Blanchard, John P. Carlos, and Alan Randolph. *The 3 Keys to Empowerment,* (San Francisco, CA: Berrett-Koehler Publishing, 2001), 22-23.

44. Albert Bandura. *Self-efficacy: The Exercise of Control.* (New York, NY: W. H. Freeman, 1997).

45. Elizabeth F. Wywialowski. *Managing Client Care*, 3rd ed. (St. Louis, MO: Mosby, 2004), 19.

46. Ken Blanchard, John P. Carlos, and Alan Randolph. *The 3 Keys to Empowerment,* (San Francisco, CA: Berrett-Koehler Publishing, 2001), 22.

47. Steven H. Woolf, Steven Jonas, and Evonne Kaplan-Liss. *Health Promotion and Disease Prevention in Clinical Practice,* 2nd ed. (Philadelphia, PA: Lippincott Williams and Wilkins, 2008), xxix.

48. Thomas Bodenheimer, Edward H. Wagner, and Kevin Grumbach. "Improving Primary Care for Patients with Chronic Illness," *JAMA* 288, no.14 (2002): 1775.

49. Michael A. Stelman. "The Integrated Summary: A Documentation Tool to Improve Patient Care," *Family Practice Management* 10, no. 4 (2003): 33.

50. Chronic Disease Electronic Management System. *CDEMS Basics*, n.d., *http://www.CDEMS.com* (accessed June 20, 2012).

51. National Health Service. *Summary Care.* (England: Crown, 2011), *http://www.nhscarerecords.nhs.uk/* (accessed February 8, 2012).

52. Jim Champy and Harry Greenspun. *Reengineering Health Care: A Manifesto for Radically Rethinking Health Care Delivery* (Upper Saddle River, NJ: Pearson Education, 2010), 72.

53. Jim Champy and Harry Greenspun. *Reengineering Health Care: A Manifesto for Radically Rethinking Health Care Delivery* (Upper Saddle River, NJ: Pearson Education, 2010), 72.

54. Paula Haas. "Medical Home Model Calls for New Payment Methods: Experimentation Is Name of the Game," *American Academy of Family Physicians*, Special Report (February 17, 2009), *http://www.aafp.org/online/en/home/publications/news/new-new/pcmh/2009217pcmhpayment.html* (accessed June 20, 2012).

55. Jeff Kullgren and Maria D. Sibella. "Calculating Your Costs Per Visit," *Family Practice Management*, no.4 (April 11, 2004): 41-45.

Chapter Four

Directed Care –
Putting the Process into Action

Directed Care is not a plug-in concept. The process must be tailored to meet specific practice characteristics. An organization, whether comprising one or several primary care clinics, must customize to fit their population base – age, chronic conditions, resources available, and reimbursement capabilities. Directed Care is not intended to operate as a free-standing service but rather as part of the primary care team for a Patient-Centered Medical Home, but is not a necessity. At a minimum, Directed Care should be attached to some form of team-based care to prevent fragmentation of services.

Roles and responsibilities of professional nurses have been modified in the Directed Care concept to a position of autonomy in wellness care with the addition of two tools for care coordination – an integrated Health Monitoring Plan and a comprehensive Summary Health Care Record. Care management is also presented with planned visits for preventive care and chronic care follow-up. The final addition for profession nurse activities in Directed Care is an evaluation activity – the assessment of utilization of health care services for each health care consumer. All four activities can be done concurrently and have been bundled and given the designation of "Check-in Visit." An organization can elect to implement only one component or another combination of the four components. The birth month of the health care consumer is recommended as the anchor month for each individual's yearly planned activities and assessments. That date is well known by the health care consumer and is listed on the health /medical records.

Health monitoring guidelines and standing orders need to be established to direct coordination of planned Wellness Visits across the life span from infancy through elder care, depending on the selected population of the practice. Recommendations from the U.S. Preventive Services Task Force, the *Bright Futures* reference by the American Academy of Pediatrics, and the Advisory Committee of Immunization Practices should be used for clinical preventive care guidelines for different age groups. Pregnancy is expected to be handled as special and set aside from the other wellness preventive care, as stated earlier. The Summary Health Care Record can have an entry for "Due" with month and year indicated for any projected intervention. Good resources to outline developmental goals, physiological changes, and anticipatory guidance for each age group are the books, *Health Promotion Throughout the Life Span*[1] by Carole Edelman and Carol Mandle and *Health Promotion Strategies Through the Life Span* by Ruth Murray, Judith Zentner, and Richard Yakimo.[2] Tools available to illustrate specific risks for an age group include the CDC charts showing *10 Leading Causes of Death by Age Group*[3] and *10 Leading Causes of Injuries by Age Group*,[4] available at the CDC website.

Self-management skill and confidence levels are evaluated at each annual visit for chronic conditions and acute minor illnesses or injuries. Coaching can be offered to assist with development of self-management to optimize the probability of early recovery or to minimize the probability of advancement of the problem. The book referenced above by Murray, Zentner, and Yakimo summarizes information for effective communication methods and interviewing approaches in a table format for any clinical team member seeking a quick review to sharpen communication skills.[5] *Health Promotion and Disease Prevention in Clinical Practice*,[6] by Steven Woolf, Steven Jonas, and Evonne Kaplan-Liss, is an excellent reference book for an upstream approach to health care services and has been cited frequently in the presentation of DIRECTED CARE.

Under the expectation that the Patient-Centered Medical Home sets the stage for health care delivery in ambulatory primary care, it is proposed that the medical staff manages the planned visits for chronic care and the professional nurses manage the planned visits for preventive care or Wellness Visits. It is anticipated that nurse practitioners would participate as health care providers for both scenarios. Referrals can be made to other professional team members, or community-based resources can be facilitated when indicated.

The role of information technology will vary from organization to organization, depending upon the population served and which communication tools will be the most effective. The key is to make the role of using information technology an evolving one. Various accessibility options would be ideal for communication between providers and health care consumers. Reimbursed encounters outside office visits will be welcomed by both the health care provider and consumer.

Health care professionals carry a responsibility to assure information is available and relevant to health issues. The Internet provides volumes of information, but the dependability of content or appropriateness of an application to a given situation may need professional nurse consultation.

Good programming of the report component for the Summary Health Care Record and accurate entries for diagnosis codes under ICD-9 or upcoming ICD-10 most applicable to the health care consumer will provide data for population management. It is recognized that professional nurses are often tasked with this non-revenue-generating activity. However, for the purpose of DIRECTED CARE, the emphasis is only on accurate recording on the Summary Health Care Record to assist with this organizational function. The Healthcare Effectiveness Data and Information Set (HEDIS) is often used as a reporting mechanism for specific preventive care elements. There are several limitations in what the numbers represent and which parameters are reported. HEDIS is a separate software program and requires non-clinical time to make separate entries for select and limited preventive care parameters. The Summary Health Care Record has the potential to serve as a multi-purpose data base.

It might be helpful to design a Check-in Visit Worksheet as a general template similar to the well-known "Pre-op Worksheet" with areas set aside to enter individual data for a given person. A checklist format can be established for workflow to cover the tasks to be accomplished during the process of the annual Check-in Visits with adjustments for individual health care consumer's age, gender, and specific issues. However, the same precaution exists for the use of templates and checklists. They have a down side in that so much time and attention are devoted to filling out the spaces or boxes that the usefulness may become overshadowed.

Pre-visit activities and activities specific for each component of the Check-in Visit are outlined in Table 4.1. The table illustrates an overview of DIRECTED CARE activities for an integrated Check-in Visit process.

Table 4.1. Check-in Visit Process

	Initial*	Annual
Preliminary Data Collection		
Solicit information from health care consumer, caregiver, or designated medical power of attorney. (Initial data collection to establish data base, orient health care consumer to the process, and initiate relative components until upcoming Birth Month.)	Request following information for past 3 years: 1 List of providers and contact information 2 Diagnostic testing results not present in records 3 ER visit information 4 Therapeutic services - OT/PT, chiropractor, massage therapist, other CAM • Conduct complexity determination for care coordination. • Acquire current age and gender preventive care recommendations. • Solicit health care consumer health concerns.	• Obtain Medical Plans of Care for each chronic illness. • Request Utilization Reports or billing information. • Obtain age and gender specific preventive care recommendations. • Solicit health care consumer concerns for upcoming year. • Confer with team members about which activities to include in Check-in Visits. • Request preventive care screening tests.

	Initial*	Annual
Wellness Check		
GOAL: Provide health promotion and disease prevention activities to reduce risk of onset or to minimize severity of disease or injury.	Obtain Comprehensive Health History: 1 Past medical history--major illness and/or injuries, operations, hospitalizations, current medications, herbals/supplements, allergies, preventive care screening tests, diagnostic testing 2 Family history 3 Social history--support systems, work activities/risks, leisure activities 4 Review of systems 5 Health practices--food choices, physical activity patterns, sleep/rest, stress management, substance use (caffeine, alcohol, drugs), environmental safety • Evaluate preventive care status--completed vs incomplete recommendations • Assess function--vision, hearing, mobility, dexterity, cognitive abilities. • Note anxiety, stress, or depressive episodes and intervention, connection to others, communication patterns. • Perform Developmental Testing as indicated. • Obtain Ht, Wt (calculate BMI), B/P. • Plan with health care consumer desired actions to bring up-to-date before next Birth Month. • Summarize findings for preventive screening and health risks. • Update immunizations as indicated.	• Update Health History. • Identify health risks. • Re-evaluate self-management skill level. • Collaborate with health care consumer about which action to take on health risks. • Assess function--vision, hearing, mobility, dexterity, cognitive abilities. • Note anxiety, stress, or depressive episodes and intervention, connection to others, communication patterns. • Perform Developmental Testing as indicated. • Solicit 24-hr Food and Beverage Intake--what, when, how much. • Obtain Ht, Wt (calculate BMI), B/P, head or waist circumference as appropriate. • Perform HME indicated by USPSTF—NP (include assessment functional impairment). • Summarize findings with health care consumer. • Solicit readiness to change personal health habits. • Collaborate action plan and record on Health Monitoring Plan. • Assess immunizations status and administer in accordance with ACIP.

	Initial*	Annual
Utilization Review		
GOAL: Evaluate health care consumer utilization patterns to provide insight for more effective or efficient individual use of health care services.	• Orient to Directed Care activities. • Ascertain knowledge of navigation through health care system and self-care of injuries and acute illnesses. • Review emergent conditions and appropriate action. • Provide information about health care consumer role and responsibilities.	• Request health care consumer provide information for any encounters outside organization. • Validate information with health care consumer. • Compare previous period utilization with Health Monitoring Plan. • Discuss variance with health care consumer.
Summary Health Care Record		
GOAL: Establish a consolidated organized data base with annual updates to facilitate optimal health status evaluation and care coordination.	• Assemble data on Summary Health Care Record. • Validate with health care consumer--obtain name and contact of all health care providers other than Primary Care Provider. • Provide copy to individual.	• Update all categories. • Provide copy to individual.
Health Monitoring Plan		
GOAL: Map health care consumer actions for a 12-month period to coordinate health care services and encourage direction toward maximal level of wellness.	Map collaborative actions, including self-management skill development and/or facilitate use of community-based resources as indicated for period until Birth Month.	• Inquire about each Medical Plan of Care-- perceived benefit, possible barriers, level of confidence to accomplish stated goal(s) . • Collaborative referral to other professional health providers as indicated--Dietician, Behavioral Health, Home Care, PT/OT, Clinical Pharmacist, Social Work, Case Management • Facilitate use of community-based resources as indicated--living environment evaluation, life event support, physical activity program, nutritional awareness, stress management, tobacco cessation, substance use, etc. • Map collaborative actions, including self-management skills development for 12-month period and sign.

*Activities can be geared for interval until Birth Month for new enrollees:

< 3months - Request Comprehensive Health History and plan/schedule initial Check-in Visit.

3-6 months - Request completed Comprehensive Health History and initiate Summary Health Care Record (with due date for Check-in Visit).

< 6 month - Request completed Comprehensive Health History, request Preventive Care incomplete screening recommendations to date, initiate Summary Health Care Record (with due date for Check-in Visit), and provide abbreviated Health Monitoring Plan.

Consulting and counseling are considered ongoing DIRECTED CARE activities, so are illustrated separately from the Check-in Visit's components in Table 4.2.

Table 4.2. On-going Professional Nurse Activities

Consulting/Advising or Counseling/Coaching Activities	
GOAL: Develop health care consumer confidence and ability for health decision making and appropriate utilization of health care services.	• Provide information for evaluating validity and reliability of health information. • Triage acute episodes. • Guide acute episodes to proper interventions. • Provide information about consequences of inaction on unfavorable health issues. • Evaluate health care consumer readiness to change. • Counsel/Coach personal behavior change. • Counsel/Coach to develop ability and confidence in self-management skills. • Guide toward effective and efficient utilization of health care system. • Develop confidence and ability for health decision making and appropriate utilization health care services.

Team Interaction

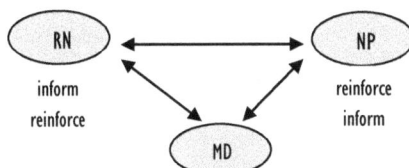

RN   NP   MD

inform
reinforce

reinforce
inform

An organization should consider a trial run of a portion of the DIRECTED CARE concept before implementation. A trial run for a small group of health care consumers without complex issues would provide an opportunity to test workflow and to evaluate problem areas before implementation for a larger group of health care consumers.

Reimbursement of DIRECTED CARE activities has two possible sources: (1) dedicated care management funds set aside for each health care consumer in a health plan either as a monthly stipend or a consumer-controlled fund such as a Health Savings Account (HSA) or (2) funds re-directed from other cost centers in an organization as has been done in some instances for case management. There is more latitude for funding the second possibility in a closed system.

Notes

1. Carole L. Edelman and Carol L. Mandle. *Health Promotion Throughout the Life Span*, 7th ed. (St Louis, MO: Mosby-Elsevier, 2009).

2. Ruth B. Murray, Judith P. Zentner, and Richard Yakimo. *Health Promotion Strategies Through the Life Span*, 8th ed. (Upper Saddle River, NJ: Prentice-Hall, 2008).

3. Centers for Disease Control and Prevention. "10 Leading Causes of Death by Age Group, United States - 2009," National Center for Injury Prevention and Control, *http://www.cdc.gov/ Injury/wisqars/pdf/10LCD-Age-Grp-US-2009-a.pdf* (accessed June 20, 2012).

4. Centers for Disease Control and Prevention. "National Estimates of 10 Leading Causes of Nonfatal Injuries Treated in Hospital Emergency Departments, United States – 2010," National Center for Injury Prevention and Control, *http://cdc.gov/Injury/ wisqars/pdf/ National_Estim_ 10_Leading_Causes_Nonfatal_ Injuries_Tx_Hospital_ED_US2010-a.pdf* (accessed June, 27, 2012).

5. Ruth B. Murray, Judith P. Zentner, and Richard Yakimo. *Health Promotion Strategies Through the Life Span*, 8th ed. (Upper Saddle River, NJ: Prentice-Hall, 2008), 47-51.

6. Steven H. Woolf, Steven Jonas, and Evonne Kaplan-Liss. *Health Promotion and Disease Prevention in Clinical Practice,* 2nd ed. (Philadelphia, PA: Lippincott Williams and Wilkins, 2008).

Chapter Five

Planning Professional Nurse Time Allocation for DIRECTED CARE Activities

The first step is projecting or forecasting workload for DIRECTED CARE activities. Retrospective (historical) data is not available for precise planning of professional nursing activities related to the concept of DIRECTED CARE. However, other similar activities of professional nurses, such as case management or care management, can be used to formulate an estimate of time requirements. These roles require primarily cognitive skills and comparably little technical skill for medical or nursing procedures.

The annual Check-in Visit will constitute the greatest time requirement for each health care consumer in DIRECTED CARE. The population served will present many variables for planning time allocation. An experienced professional nurse with expertise in ambulatory primary care will be valuable in dealing with these variations. Factors affecting time allocation are:

- Number of health issues – positive health risks, number of chronic conditions
- Availability of data – inside or outside organization
- Clarity and organization of data
- Recommendations for preventive care concurrent with age and gender
- Presence of communication impairment
- Requirement for other health care decision makers

Most models for ambulatory nursing workload measurement are components of staffing models adapted from the acute care setting.[1] A literature search found a discussion on the Workload Measurement and Reporting System (WMRS),[2] which is still under development. In the discussion on the WMRS there was difficulty in estimating the time it took to complete an activity due to the frequent work interruptions in the ambulatory care setting, and refinement of the system has continued.

The DIRECTED CARE process will encompass planning for a combination of administrative and paid time off (non-productive time) in addition to the clinical time (productive time). Administrative time is commonly figured as part of overhead, and clinical time represents time that could be charged for reimbursement. Management's challenge is to control the amount of administrative time for cost control. The Washington State Blue Ribbon Commission stated in their report, after evaluating administrative health care costs: "Any dollar spent on administrative overhead is a dollar not available for patient care."[3] Could a portion of administrative funds be re-allocated to care management, including DIRECTED CARE activities?

It is anticipated that the establishment of the Summary Health Care Record and Health Monitoring Plan will require the greatest time allotment for the Check-in Visits. The expertise of the professional nurse is not required for all aspects of the process. The task of requesting information is a clerical task. However, the determination of what information is needed and from whom falls within the responsibility of the professional nurse.

A rough estimate of time for a given health care consumer can be projected with flexibility to add or subtract time as indicated. Planning factors, such as projected time frames for age group and individual complexity determination beforehand, allows greater control. Time studies need to be conducted to be more precise. The health care consumer can assist with data collection once the type of information and the time frame when the information is needed have been outlined. This will promote active health care consumer participation and self-management.

Allotting time for an independent professional nurse activity can be augmented by conducting a complexity determination for coordinating care. A complexity determination will provide assistance in allocating time for an individual health care consumer. The value of this approach is also seen in relationship to the Patient-Centered Medical Home. An individual complexity determination contributes to making interactions with health care consumers truly patient-centered.[4] The Minnesota Complexity Assessment Method discussed in *Primary Care for Patient Complexity, Not Only Disease*[5] is mostly designed to assess the complexity of one medical condition. The sample tool in Table 5.1 was adapted for overall care coordination for a health care consumer. Elements about specific interventions, such as changing personal health behaviors, are not included on this form. Health care consumers present a unique set of circumstances for coordination of health services. Getting a grasp on the factors that affect time allocation will be beneficial.

Table 5.1. Complexity Determination for Care Coordination

Complexity Factor Levels	Score Level
A. Number unstable/uncontrolled chronic conditions None = Level 0 1 = Level 2 2 = Level 4 3 = Level 6 4 = Level 8	
B. Number stable/controlled chronic conditions None = Level 0 1 = Level 1 2 = Level 2 3 = Level 3 4 = Level 4 5 = Level 5	
C. Number providers other than PCM, including Medical Specialist, Behavioral Health, Case Management, to manage medical condition(s) None = Level 0 1 = Level 1 2 = Level 2 3 = Level 3 4 = Level 4 5 = Level 5	
D. Barriers to communication (scored level based on severity)	
Cognitive impairment None = Level 0----------------------------------Marked = Level 5	
Vision impairment None = Level 0----------------------------------Marked = Level 5	
Hearing impairment None = Level 0----------------------------------Marked = Level 5	
Low literacy level None = Level 0----------------------------------Marked = Level 5	
English speaking Yes = Level 0 Limited = Level 3 No = Level 5	

Complexity Factor Levels	Score Level
E. Engagement and participation in managing own health care Level 0 = High Level 1 = Moderately High Level 2 = Moderate Level 3 = Moderately Low Level 4 = Low Level 5 = None	
F. Dependent on caregiver (scored level based on degree of care coordination required through others) None = Level 0--- Always = Level 5	
G. Resources available	
Intact support system Level 0 = Strong --- None = Level 5	
Financial limitation Level 0 = None--- Always = Level 5	
Transportation limitation Level 0 = None---Always = Level 5	
Communication capability	
Phone Yes = Level 0 No = Level 5	
Email Yes = Level 0 No = Level 3	
U.S. Mail Yes = Level 0 No = Level 4	
TOTAL	

Complexity Level	Total Scored Level Range
Low Moderately Low Moderate High Extensive	(to be determined)

Combining the unit of service with the Complexity Determination for Care Coordination could look like the following sample in Table 5.2. The numbers in this table are for illustration purposes only. They do not represent a given clinical situation.

Table 5.2. Units of Service Example for Annual Check-In Visit with Moderate Complexity

Activity	RN Indirect	Direct	Sub Total	NP
Preliminary	2.5	1.0	3.5	---
Wellness	1.0	2.0	3.0	0.5
Utilization Review	1.5	0.5	2.0	---
Summary Health Care Record	1.5	0.5	2.0	---
Health Monitoring Plan	1.0	0.5	1.5	0.5
TOTAL	7.5	4.5	12.0	1.0

NP column notes: **Evaluation/Management Comprehensive Preventive Medicine**

CPT Codes*
New 99381-99387
Established 99391-99397
[Well Baby 99381 & 99391]
Add other Procedure codes as appropriate.
Includes counseling and/or anticipatory guidance and/or risk factor reduction intervention which are provided at the time of initial or periodic comprehensive examination.

Subtract units of services for lower Complexity Level
Add units of services for higher Complexity Level

*Age and gender appropriate history/exam. Not accepted by Medicare.
(American Medical Association *CPT 2012 Common Procedural Terminology*)

NOTE: NP time allocation for units of service does not include activities listed under CPT codes.

There are multiple unique characteristics in an ambulatory primary care setting. Experienced ambulatory care professional nurses can estimate time with a degree of accuracy for a given clinical situation. The best means for true accuracy are time studies. Clerical tasks are not included in determination of time requirement for professional nurse activities but do need to be addressed separately. It is suggested that units of services be used for these activities in the future. The proficiency of team members performing DIRECTED CARE activities will increase as the workflow becomes established, and the units of service may need adjustment. Time allocation is also subject to the experience level of the individual performing the task.

Time management for DIRECTED CARE activities will be less complicated than activities in acute settings, since DIRECTED CARE is primarily structured with scheduled events. Except for a possible episodic (acute)

consulting request or triage, the majority of activities will be prospective, and time allocation can be controlled. How episodic consulting calls or requests are handled will be a management decision. The goal for DIRECTED CARE workload management is appropriate time allocation to maximize efficiency for professional time utilization and concurrently provide health care consumer access to services for "getting healthy and staying healthy."

Matching workload to available professional nurse time is presented in Appendix N. Time for nurse practitioners engaged in DIRECTED CARE activities is mixed with units of service and estimated time to conduct procedures designated by CPT codes. The workload reflected in DIRECTED CARE activities places professional nurses in a position of autonomy with the opportunity to maximize their scope of practice and to make valued contributions as an inter-disciplinary team member.

Notes

1. Beth Ann Swan and Karen F. Griffin. "Measuring Nurse Workload in Ambulatory Care," *Nursing Economics* 23, no.5 (2005): 258.

2. Katherine L. Dickson, Angela M. Cramer, and Colleen M. Peckham. "Nursing Workload Measurement in Ambulatory Care," *Nursing Economics* 28, no.1 (2010): 42.

3. Washington Blue Ribbon Commission. *Health Care Administrative Expense Analysis: Blue Ribbon Commission Recommendation 6 Final Report* (Olympia, WA: Washington State Office of Insurance Commissioner, 2007), 3.

4. C. J. Peek, Macaran A. Baird, and Eli Coleman. "Primary Care for Patient Complexity, Not Only Disease," *Families, Systems, & Health* 27, no. 4 (2009): 291.

5. C. J. Peek, Macaran A. Baird, and Eli Coleman. "Primary Care for Patient Complexity, Not Only Disease," *Families, Systems, & Health* 27, no. 4 (2009): 287-302.

Chapter Six

Closing Remarks

DIRECTED CARE complements the Patient-Centered Medical Home model and targets re-engineering portions of the health care delivery system to improve effectiveness and efficiency for cost containment and health improvement for health care consumers. Professional nurse activities in DIRECTED CARE are expected to maintain congruence with:

- PCMH Joint Principles
- ANA Nursing Scope and Standards of Practice
- NONPF and AACN Nurse Practitioner Primary Care Competencies
- AAACN Scope and Standards of Practice for Professional Ambulatory Care Nursing
- Medicare Annual Wellness Visit Guidelines

What remains to be seen is which components of the Affordable Care Act will remain viable after scrutiny of Congress in light of the U.S. Supreme Court ruling. The undisputed fact is the current health care system is not sustainable.

Under the Patient-Centered Medical Home model, health care consumers will be allowed some control in health care decision making. DIRECTED CARE can collaborate with health care consumers and map a journey toward optimal wellness. This guidance will be enhanced with a collective plan developed by other professional team members for illness care at all stages. The process becomes shared care management.

The roles and responsibilities of professional nurses in DIRECTED CARE are in unison with a statement from the Institute of Medicine (IOM) 2010 report, *The Future of Nursing: Leading Change, Advancing Health.* The IOM envisions the future with "primary care and prevention as the central drivers of the health care system. Inter-professional collaboration and coordination are the norm. Payment for health care rewards value, not volume of services, and quality care is provided at a price that is affordable for both individual and society."[1] There is economic value in DIRECTED CARE activities by professional nurses to prevent:

- Fragmentation or duplication of health care services
- Occurrence of behavior-related diseases
- Exacerbations of disease attributed to lack of self-management skills
- Injury from unsafe environments
- Occurrence of vaccine-preventable disease
- Progression of injury complications or disease escalations without early intervention
- High utilization of health care resources

Procedures and the science of medicine have had a long presence in what appears to be unquestioned reimbursement. It will take time to re-establish the value of the art of medicine and nursing in which talking and relationships will have the same value to health care consumers as they did when consumers were the main direct payer for services.

Reimbursement of services for all practice settings may be the largest obstacle for full implementation of the DIRECTED CARE concept. Policy makers are currently evaluating alternatives to fee-for-service that rewards volume. Strategies are being developed for reimbursement that values indirect care elements. Proper reimbursement is required for time to address health care needs in patient-centered care in order to make interventions relevant to an individual and to coordinate care to provide continuity. When health care consumers receive quality care at the right time, for the right service, with the right provider, and at a reasonable and fair reimbursement for providers, all will be winners in a professional team-based service.

In words taken from the IOM *Future of Nursing* report cited above, DIRECTED CARE with professional nurses on point will be –

Leading Change, Advancing Health

Notes

1.	Institute of Medicine. *The Future of Nursing: Leading Change, Advancing Health (Summary)*, (Washington, DC: National Academy Press, 2010), S-1.

Bibliography

American Academy of Ambulatory Care Nursing. *Scope and Standards of Practice for Professional Ambulatory Care Nursing*, 8th ed. Pitman, NJ: Jannetti, 2010.

American Academy of Nursing. *The Health Care Home Debate: Opportunities for Nursing*. Washington, DC, 2008.
http://www.pcpcc.net/files/healthhomepaperFINAL.0608.doc
(accessed June 20, 2012).

American Nurses Association. *Nursing Scope and Standards of Practice*, 2nd ed. Silver Spring, MD: Nursebooks.org, 2010.

Bandura, Albert. *Self-efficacy: The Exercise of Control*. New York: W. H. Freeman, 1997.

Blanchard, Ken, John P. Carlos, and Alan Randolph. *The 3 Keys to Empowerment*. San Francisco, CA: Berrett-Koehler Publishing, 2001.

Bodenheimer, Thomas. "Coordinating Care: A Major (Unreimbursed) Task of Primary Care" (editorial). *Annals of Internal Medicine* 147, no. 10 (2007): 730-731.

Bodenheimer, Thomas, Kate Lorig, Halsted Holman, and Kevin Grumbach. "Patient Self-Management of Chronic Disease in Primary Care." *JAMA* 288, no. 19 (2002): 2469-2475.

Bodenheimer, Thomas, Edward H. Wagner, and Kevin Grumbach. "Improving Primary Care for Patients with Chronic Illness." *JAMA* 288, no. 14 (2002): 1775-1779.

Borrelli, Belinda. "Using Motivational Interviewing to Promote Behavior Change and Enhance Health." *Public Health Nursing* 18, no. 3 (2001): 178-185.

Botelho, Richard J. *Motivational Practice: Promoting Healthy Habits and Self-care of Chronic Disease*. Rochester, NY: MHH Publications, 2004.

Carver, M. Colette, and Anne T. Jessie. "Patient-Centered Care in a Medical Home." *OJIN: The Online Journal of Issues in Nursing* 16, no. 2 (2001): Manuscript 4.

Center for Health Care Strategies. "Care Management Definition and Framework," 2007. *http://www.chcs.org/publications3960/publications_show.html?doc_id=58183* (accessed June 27, 2012).

Center for Health Transformation. *Healthcare Consumerism: The Basis of a 21ˢᵗ Century Intelligent Health System*, 2006. *http://www.healthcarevisions.net/f/2006_Healthcare_ Consumerism_CHT.pdf* (accessed June 20, 2012).

Centers for Disease Control and Prevention. "Chronic Diseases: The Power to Prevent, The Call to Control". National Center for Chronic Disease Prevention and Health Promotion, (2009). *http://www.cdc.gov/chronicdisease/resources/publications/AAG/pdf/chronic.pdf* (accessed July 3, 2012).

Centers for Medicare and Medicaid Services (CMS). "Annual Wellness Visit Benefit Overview," 2011. *http://www.cms.gov/Outreach-and-Education/Medicare-Learning-Network-MLN/MLNProducts/ downloads/ mps_guide_web-061305.pdf* (accessed June 20, 2012).

Champy, Jim, and Harry Greenspun. *Reengineering Health Care: A Manifesto for Radically Rethinking Health Care Delivery*. Upper Saddle River, NJ: Pearson Education, 2010.

Chiverton, Patricia A., Kathryn M. Votava, and Donna M. Tortoretti. "The Future Role of Nursing in Health Promotion." *American Journal of Health Promotion* 18, no. 2 (2003): 192-194.

Chronic Disease Electronic Management System. *Data Entry Guide*. 2011. *http://www.CDEMS.com* (accessed May 23, 2012).

Chronic Disease Electronic Management System. *Reports Guide*. 2011.
   http://www.CDEMS.com (accessed May 23, 2012).

Chronic Disease Electronic Management System. *CDEMS Basics*. n.d.
   http://www.CDEMS.com (accessed June 20, 2012).

Cohen, Seth, Kurt D. Grote, Wayne E. Pietraszek, and Francois LaFlamme.
   "Increasing Consumerism in Healthcare Through Intelligent
   Information Technology." *The American Journal of Managed Care* 16,
   Special Edition (2010): SP37-SP43.

Commonweath Fund. *U.S. Spends Far More for Health Care than 12
   Industrialized Nations, but Quality Varies*. May 3, 2012.
   *http://www.commonwealthfund.org/News/News-Release/2012/May/US-Spends-Far-
   More-for-Health-Care-Than-12-Industrialized-Nations-but-Quality-Varies.aspx*
   (accessed July 3, 2012).

Courson, Sara. *What is Telephone Triage?* 2005.
   http://www.connectionmagazine.com/articles/5/090.html
   (accessed June 20, 2012).

"CPT 2012: Common Procedural Terminology, Professional Edition."
   American Medical Association, 2011.

Davies, Karen, Cathy Sohoen, and Kristof Sromikis. *"Mirror, Mirror on the
   Wall. How the Performance of the U.S. Health Care System Compares
   Internationally. 2010 Update.* Commonwealth Fund, no. 1400
   (2010).
   *http://www.commonwealth.org/~/media/Files/Publications/Fund%20Report/
   2010/Jun/1400_Davis_Mirror_Mirror_on_the_wall_2010.pdf*
   (accessed July 3, 2012).

Dickson, Katherine L., Angela M. Cramer, and Colleen M. Peckham.
   "Nursing Workload Measurement in Ambulatory Care." *Nursing
   Economics* 28, no. 1 (2010): 37-43.

Edelman, Carole L., and Carol L. Mandle. *Health Promotion Throughout the
   Life Span*, 7th ed. St Louis, MO: Mosby-Elsevier, 2009.

Farquhar, John W. *The American Way of Life Need Not Be Hazardous to Your Health*. Reading, MA: Addison-Wesley Publishing, 1987.

Fellows of the American Academy of Nurse Practitioner Invitational Think Tank. "Nurse Practitioners: Promoting Access to Coordinated Primary Care." Washington, DC: American Academy of Nurse Practitioners Office of Public Policy, December 5, 2007.

Fries, James F., C. Everett Koop, Jacque Sokolov, Carson E. Beadle, and Daniel Wright. "Beyond Health Promotion: Reducing Need and Demand for Medical Care." *Health Affairs* 17, no. 2 (1998): 70-80.

Garnica, Mary P. "Coordinated Primary Care ('Medical Home' Model)." *Clinical Scholars Review* 2, no. 2 (2009): 60-64.

Goldstein, Douglas E. *e-Healthcare: Harness the Power of Internet e-Commerce and e-Care*. Gaithersburg, MD: Aspen Publishers, 2000.

Green, Lawrence W. "Health Promotion Policy and the Placement of Responsibility for Personal Health Care. "*Family and Community Health* 3, no. 3 (1979): 51-64.

Haas, Paula. "Medical Home Model Calls for New Payment Methods: Experimentation Is Name of the Game." American Academy of Family Physicians (Special Report) February 17, 2009. *http://www.aafp.org/online/en/home/publications/news/news-now/pcmh/ 2009217pcmhpayment.html* (accessed June 20, 2012).

Hagan, Joseph F., Judith Shaw, and Paula M. Duncan, eds. *Bright Futures: Guidelines for Health Supervision of Infants, Children and Adolescents*, 3rd ed. Elk Grove Village, IL: American Academy of Pediatrics. 2008. *http://brightfutures.aap.org/pdfs/3rd-Edition-Guidelines-and-Pocket-Guide.html* (accessed July 18, 2012).

Hayes, Eileen, and Karen A. Kalmakis. "From the Sidelines: Coaching as a Nurse Practitioner Strategy for Improving Health Outcomes." *Journal of the American Academy of Nurse Practitioners* 19 (2007): 555-562.

Huffman, Melina. "Health Coaching: A New and Exciting Technique to Enhance Patient Self- Management and Improve Outcomes." *Home Healthcare Nurse* 25, no. 4 (2007): 271-274.

Institute for the Future. *Health and Health Care 2010: The Forecast, The Challenge*, 2nd ed. Princeton, NJ: Jossey-Bass, 2003.

Institute for Healthcare Improvement. "Building an Effective Planned Care System for All Patients in Ambulatory Settings." *Planned Care Guide.* n.d. *http://www.ihi.org* (accessed June 20, 2012).

Institute of Medicine. *Crossing the Quality Chasm: A New Health System for the 21st Century.* Washington, DC: National Academy Press, 2001.

Institute of Medicine. *The Future of Nursing: Leading Change, Advancing Health (Summary).* Washington, DC: National Academy Press, 2010.

Kabcenell, Andrea I., Jerry Langley, and Cindy Hupke. *Innovations in Planned Care. IHI Innovation Series White Papers.* Cambridge, MA: Institute for Healthcare Improvement, 2006.

Klein, Ezra. "Administrative Costs in Health Care: A Primer". *The Washington Post* (July 7, 2009). *http://voices.washingtonpost.com/ezra-klein/2009/07/ administrative_costs_ in_health.html* (accessed May 23, 2012).

Kullgren, Jeff, and Maria D. Sibella. "Calculating Your Costs Per Visit." *Family Practice Management*, no. 4 (April 11, 2004): 41-45.

Leavell, Hugh R., and E. Gurney Clark. *Preventive Medicine for the Doctor in His Community*, 2nd ed. New York, NY: McGraw-Hill, 1965.

Lee, Thomas H., and Robert A. Berenson. "The Organization of Health Care Delivery: A Roadmap for Accelerated Improvement" Chap. 2 in *The Health Care Delivery System: A Blueprint for Reform* Washington, DC: Center for American Progress and the Institute on Medicine as a Profession, 2008. *http://www.americanprogress.org/issues/healthcare/report/2008/10/3/5129/ the-health-care-delivery-system-a-blueprint-for-reform/* (accessed June 20, 2012).

Mataconis, Doug. *Health Care Costs and the Third Party Payer Problem.* (June 8, 2011). *http://www.outsidethebeltway.com/health-care-costs-and-the-third-party-payer-problem/* (accessed February 10, 2012).

McGinnis, J. Michael. "Forward" in *Health Promotion and Disease Prevention in Clinical Practice. Health Promotion and Disease Prevention in Clinical Practice,* 2nd ed. Philadelphia, PA: Lippincott Williams and Wilkins, 2008.

Murray, Ruth B., Judith P. Zentner, and Richard Yakimo. *Health Promotion Strategies Through the Life Span,* 8th ed. Upper Saddle River, NJ: Prentice-Hall, 2008.

National Business Group on Health. *Payment Systems, Government Policies and Market Incentives Should Refocus Efforts on Disease Prevention.* Washington, DC (2010). *http://www.businessgrouphealth.org/pdfs/preventioncarepositionstatement.pdf* (accessed June 20, 2012).

National Health Service. *Summary Care.* England: Crown. 2011. *http://www.nhscarerecords.nhs.uk/* (accessed February 8, 2012).

National Organization of Nurse Practitioner Faculties (NONPF) and American Association of Colleges of Nursing (AACN). *Nurse Practitioner Primary Care Competencies in Specialty Areas: Adult, Family, Gerontological, Pediatric, and Women's Health.* Rockville, MD: Department of Health and Human Services. 2002. *http://www.aacn.nche.edu/education-resources/npcompetencies.pdf.* (accessed June 20, 2012).

Noar, Seth M., Nancy G. Harrington, Stephanie K. Van Stee, and Rosalie S. Aldrich. "Tailored Health Communication to Change Lifestyle Behavior." *American Journal of Lifestyle Medicine* 5, no. 2 (2001): 112-122.

No Time to Teach Blog. "Patient Education Means Information Sharing AND Coaching." March 28, 2011. *http://www.notimetoteach.com/2011/twolevels/* (accessed June 20, 2012).

Palmer, Stephen, Irene Tubbs, and Alison Whybrow. "Health Coaching to Facilitate the Promotion of Healthy Behavior and Achievement of Health-Related Goals." *International Journal of Health Promotion & Education* 4, no. 3 (2003): 91-93.

Parkinson, Michael D. *Consumer-Driven Healthcare: Prevention, Evidence-Based Care and Better Patient-Physician Relationships.* Alexandria, VA: Lumenos. n.d. *http://www.acpm.org/resource/resmgr/perpectives-files/ perspectives_Consumer_Driven.pdf* (accessed June 20, 2012).

Patient-Centered Primary Care Collaborative. *Joint Principles of Patient-Centered Medical Home* (March 2007). *http://www.pcpcc.net/joint-principles* (accessed June 20, 2012).

Patient-Centered Primary Care Collaborative. *Reimbursement Reform. A New Physician Payment System to Support Higher Quality, Lower Cost Care Through a Patient-Centered Medical Home* (May 2007). *http://www.pcpcc.net/content/reimbursement-reform-1* (accessed June 20, 2012).

Peek, C. J., Macaran A. Baird, and Eli Coleman. "Primary Care for Patient Complexity, Not Only Disease." *Families, Systems, & Health* 27, no. 4 (2009): 287-302.

Pender, Nola J., Carolyn L. Murdaugh, and Mary Ann Parsons. *Health Promotion in Nursing Practice*, 6th ed. Boston, MA: Pearson, 2011.

Redwood, Heinz. *Patient Education: The End of One-way Traffic.* April 22, 2004. *http://healthandage.com/patient-education-the-end-of-one-way-traffic* (accessed June 20, 2012).

Rimer, Barbara K., and Matthew W. Kreuter. "Advancing Tailored Communication: A Persuasion and Message Effects Perspective." *Journal of Communication* 56, Supplement (2006): S184-S201.

Schroeder, Carole A., Barbara Trehearne, and Debbie Ward. "Expanded Role of Nursing in Ambulatory Managed Care. Part I. Literature, Role Development and Justification." *Nursing Economics* 18, no. 1 (2000): 14-19.

Schroeder, Carole A., Barbara Trehearne, and Debbie Ward. "Expanded Role of Nursing in Ambulatory Managed Care. Part II. Impact on Outcomes of Costs, Quality, Provider and Patient Satisfaction." *Nursing Economics* 18, no. 2 (2000): 71-78.

Sebelius, Kathleen. "This June, Get Healthy, Stay Healthy." *Healthcare Blog.* Department of Health and Human Services (June 06, 2011) *http://www.healthcare.gov/blog/2011/06/ prevention062011a.* (accessed September 9, 2012).

Sennett, Cary, and Katie Starkey. *Measuring and Improving Efficiency in Healthcare: Report from an ABIM Foundation/IOM Meeting.* Philadelphia, PA: ABIM Foundation, 2006.

Stelman, Michael A. "The Integrated Summary: A Documentation Tool to Improve Patient Care." *Family Practice Management* 10, no. 4 (2003): 33-39.

Street, Richard L., Jr., Gregory Makoul, Neeraj K. Arora, and Ronald M. Epstein. "How Does Communication Heal? Pathways Linking Clinician-Patient Communication to Health Outcomes." *Patient Education and Counseling* 74, (2009): 295-301.

Street, Richard L., Jr. "Healing Communication: Clinician-Patient Communication." Psychosocial Health Podcast (June 13, 2011). *http://www.healthpodcasts.blogspot.com/2011/06/healing-communication-clinican-patient.htm* (accessed June 20, 2012).

Swan, Beth Ann, and Karen F. Griffin.. "Measuring Nurse Workload in Ambulatory Care." *Nursing Economics* 23, no. 5 (2005): 253-260.

Swan, Beth Ann, Regina Conway-Phillips, and Karen F. Griffin. "Demonstrating the Value of the RN in Ambulatory Care." *Nursing Economics* 24, no. 6 (2006): 315-322.

The Segal Company. *Consumerism in Health Care: The Quest to Create New Partnerships for Responsibility and Accountability* (Executive Letter). New York, NY: The Segal Group, June 2003.

Trinite, Tricia, Carol Loveland-Cherry, and Lucy Marion. "The U.S. Preventive Service Task Force: An Evidence-Based Preventive Resource for Nurse Practitioners." *Journal of American Academy of Nurse Practitioners* 21, (2009): 301-306.

U.S. Department of Health and Human Services. *The Guide to Clinical Preventive Services 2010-2111*. Agency for Healthcare Research and Quality, AHRQ Pub. No 10-0545, 2010.

Washington Blue Ribbon Commission, *Health Care Administrative Expense Analysis: Blue Ribbon Commission Recommendation 6 Final Report*, Olympia, WA: Washington State Office of Insurance Commissioner, 2007.

Weston, Marla J. "Strategies for Enhancing Autonomy and Control Over Nursing Practice." *OJIN: The Online Journal of Issues in Nursing* 15, no. 1 (2010). Manuscript 2.

Woolf, Steven H., Steven Jonas, and Evonne Kaplan-Liss. *Health Promotion and Disease Prevention in Clinical Practice*, 2nd ed. Philadelphia, PA: Lippincott Williams and Wilkins, 2008.

Wywialowski, Elizabeth F. *Managing Client Care*, 3rd ed. St. Louis, MO: Mosby, 2004.

Zimmerman, Gretchen L., Cynthia G. Olsen, and Michael F. Bosworth. "A 'Stages of Change' Approach to Helping Patients Change Behavior." *American Family Physicians* 61, no. 5 (2000): 1409-1416.

Appendix A

Joint Principles of the Patient-Centered Medical Home

American Academy of Family Physicians (AAFP)
American Academy of Pediatrics (AAP)
American College of Physicians (ACP)
American Osteopathic Association (AOA)
February 2007

Introduction

The Patient-Centered Medical Home (PCMH) is an approach to providing comprehensive primary care for children, youth and adults. The PCMH is a health care setting that facilitates partnerships between individual patients, and their personal physicians, and when appropriate, the patient's family.

The AAP, AAFP, ACP, and AOA, representing approximately 333,000 physicians, have developed the following joint principles to describe the characteristics of the PCMH.

Principles

Personal physician

Each patient has an ongoing relationship with a personal physician trained to provide first contact, continuous and comprehensive care.

Physician directed medical practice

The personal physician leads a team of individuals at the practice level who collectively take responsibility for the ongoing care of patients.

Whole person orientation

The personal physician is responsible for providing for all the patient's health care needs or taking responsibility for appropriately arranging care with other qualified professionals. This includes care for all stages of life; acute care; chronic care; preventive services; and end of life care.

Care is coordinated and/or integrated

Care is coordinated and/or integrated across all elements of the complex health care system (e.g., subspecialty care, hospitals, home health agencies, nursing homes) and the patient's community (e.g., family, public and private community-based services). Care is facilitated by registries, information technology, health information exchange and other means to assure that patients get the indicated care when and where they need and want it in a culturally and linguistically appropriate manner.

Quality and Safety

Quality and safety are hallmarks of the medical home:

- Practices advocate for their patients to support the attainment of optimal, patient-centered outcomes that are defined by a care planning process driven by a compassionate, robust partnership between physicians, patients, and the patient's family.
- Evidence-based medicine and clinical decision-support tools guide decision making.
- Physicians in the practice accept accountability for continuous quality improvement through voluntary engagement in performance measurement and improvement.

- Patients actively participate in decision-making and feedback is sought to ensure patients' expectations are being met.
- Information technology is utilized appropriately to support optimal patient care, performance measurement, patient education, and enhanced communication.
- Practices go through a voluntary recognition process by an appropriate non-governmental entity to demonstrate that they have the capabilities to provide patient centered services consistent with the medical home model.
- Patients and families participate in quality improvement activities at the practice level.

Enhanced access

Enhanced access to care is available through systems such as open scheduling, expanded hours and new options for communication between patients, their personal physician, and practice staff.

Payment

Payment appropriately recognizes the added value provided to patients who have a patient-centered medical home. The payment structure should be based on the following framework:

- It should reflect the value of physician and non-physician staff patient-centered care management work that falls outside of the face-to-face visit.
- It should pay for services associated with coordination of care both within a given practice and between consultants, ancillary providers, and community resources.
- It should support adoption and use of health information technology for quality improvement.
- It should support provision of enhanced communication access such as secure e-mail and telephone consultation.
- It should recognize the value of physician work associated with remote monitoring of clinical data using technology.

- It should allow for separate fee-for-service payments for face-to-face visits. (Payments for care management services that fall outside of the face-to-face visit, as described above, should not result in a reduction in the payments for face-to-face visits).

- It should recognize case mix differences in the patient population being treated within the practice.

- It should allow physicians to share in savings from reduced hospitalizations associated with physician-guided care management in the office setting.

- It should allow for additional payments for achieving measurable and continuous quality improvements.

Source: *Patient-Centered Primary Care Collaborative* (February 2007), http://www.pcpcc.net/ joint-principles

Appendix B

American Nurses Association (ANA) Summary of Standards for Professional Nursing Practice

The standards by which professional nurses are expected to practice in the United States are primarily established by the American Nurses Association. These standards of practice apply to all nurses at all times regardless of their role. They provide a framework for developing competencies and outline practice expectations of the professional nurse. These standards of practice form a legal reference for determining what professional nurse actions are reasonable and prudent. In essence, the main purpose for these standards is to promote, guide, and direct the practice of professional nurses.

STANDARDS OF PRACTICE

The group of standards describes the competency level of professional nurses demonstrated by utilization of the nursing process elements.

Standard 1. *Assessment*

The registered nurse collects comprehensive data pertinent to the health care consumer's health and/or the situation.

Standard 2. *Diagnosis*

The registered nurse analyzes the assessment data to determine the diagnoses or the issues.

Standard 3. *Outcomes Identification*

The registered nurse identifies expected outcomes for a plan individualized to the health care consumer or the situation.

Standard 4. *Planning*

The registered nurse develops a plan that prescribes strategies and alternatives to attain expected outcomes.

Standard 5. *Implementation*

The registered nurse implements the identified plan.

Standard 5A. *Coordination of Care*

The registered nurse coordinates care delivery.

Standard 5B. *Health Teaching and Health Promotion*

The registered nurse employs strategies to promote health and a safe environment.

Standard 5C. *Consultation*

The graduate-level prepared advanced practice registered nurse provides consultation to influence the identified plan, enhance the ability of others, and effect change.

Standard 5D. *Prescription Authority and Treatment*

The advanced practice registered nurse uses prescriptive authority, procedures, referrals, treatments, and therapies in accordance with state and federal laws and regulations.

Standard 6. *Evaluation*

The registered nurse evaluates progress toward attainment of outcomes.

STANDARDS OF PROFESSIONAL PERFORMANCE
This group of standards describes the competency level of professional behavior in the practice of nursing.

Standard 7. *Ethics*

The registered nurse practices ethically.

Standard 8. *Education*

The registered nurse attains knowledge and competence that reflect current nursing practice.

Standard 9. *Evidence-Based Practice and Research*

The registered nurse integrates evidence and research findings into practice.

Standard 10. *Quality of Practice*

The registered nurse contributes to quality nursing practice.

Standard 11. *Communication*

The registered nurse communicates effectively in all areas of practice.

Standard 12. *Leadership*

The registered nurse demonstrates leadership in the professional practice setting and the profession.

Standard 13. *Collaboration*

The registered nurse collaborates with the health care consumer, family, and others in the conduct of nursing practice.

Standard 14. *Professional Practice Evaluation*

The registered nurse evaluates her or his own nursing practice in relation to professional practice standards and guidelines, relevant statues, rules, and regulations.

Standard 15. *Resource Utilization*

The registered nurse utilizes appropriate resources to plan and provides nursing services that are safe, effective, and financially responsible.

Standard 16. *Environmental Health*

The registered nurse practices in an environmentally safe and healthy manner.

Source: American Nurses Association. *Nursing Scope and Standards of Practice*. 2nd ed. (Silver Spring, MD: Nursebooks.org, 2010), 9-11.

Each Standard of Practice for professional nurses is described in extensive detail in the referenced book and will clarify the competency level expected for each standard including specific competency levels for nurse practitioners.

Appendix C

Disease Prevention

"An ounce of prevention is worth a pound of cure"

Disease is a particular destructive process in an organ or organism with a specific cause and characteristic symptoms (Webster). Prevention is targeted toward decreasing the probability of occurrence. Once a disease does occur, measures are instituted by the health care consumer and medical care provider to arrest the disease process or minimize the risk of complications.

| PRIMARY | | SECONDARY | | TERTIARY |
| *Minimize risk for occurrence of disease* | | *Reduce risk of disease progressing* | | *Manage risk of complications* |
Health Promotion & Education	Health Protection	Early Diagnosis	Prompt & Adequate Treatment	Rehabilitation & Disability Limitation
Strive for a healthy life-style.	Make healthy food choices:	Monitor your weight and take action for excess weigh–set reasonable weight level.	**EMERGENCIES**	Follow medical plan of care—be active participant in its development.
Be knowledgeable of respiratory irritants.	• Watch intake of refined sugar.		*Get immediate medical care for:*	
	• Limit salt intake to 2400 mg/day.	Get screening laboratory tests for:	• Any potential poison exposure	Schedule periodic medical follow-up for chronic disease conditions.
Know how to protect yourself against exposure to biological agents.	• Avoid fried foods.	• Cholesterol	• Allergic reaction to an insect bite or chemicals	
	• Eat a variety of foods--include fruits and vegetables	• Fasting blood glucose	• Blood in stool or black, tar-like stool	Develop self-management skills to control chronic disease and prevent complications, including hospitalization for out-of-control disease.
Be knowledgeable of health issues/risks for out-of-country travel areas.	• Eat 3 meals/day evenly spaced.	Schedule examinations and/or procedures appropriate for age and gender:	• Blood in urine	
	• Watch portion size.		• Coughing up blood	
Know your cardiovascular and cancer risks.	Get at least 30 minutes moderate intensity physical activity each day.	• Periodic health maintenance exam	• Feeling very hot and confused after being in the heat	
	Aim for a body mass index (BMI) less than 27.	• Pelvic exam	• Difficulty breathing or feeling of choking	
	Get a health risk analysis.	• Mammogram	• Tightness, pressure, or pain in chest that spreads to neck, jaw arm or back	
	Provide indoor air quality--	• Sigmoidoscopy	• Stiff neck with fever	
	• Control dust	• Rectal exam	• Sudden loss of vision	
	• Eliminate smoke	• Eye exam for glaucoma and retinopathy	• Very bad pain anywhere on body	
	• Avoid carbon monoxide hazards	Do self-examinations:	• Vomiting up blood or what looks like coffee grounds	
	Use fragrances prudently.	• Skin	• Weakness or dizziness	
	Use all chemical agents	• Testicle	• Been out in cold and potential cold injury	
		• Breast		

| PRIMARY | | SECONDARY | | TERTIARY |
| Minimize risk for occurrence of disease | | Reduce risk of disease progressing | | Manage risk of complications |
Health Promotion & Education	Health Protection	Early Diagnosis	Prompt & Adequate Treatment	Rehabilitation & Disability Limitation
	according to manufacturer's instructions and use appropriate personal protective items.	Contact medical care provider if unplanned changes in activities of daily living are noted.	Have injectable adrenalin anaphylactic "bee sting kit" available for food and insect allergies that cause breathing problems.	
	Always cover a cough or sneeze and instruct others to do the same.		Perform appropriate self-care for:	
	Avoid tobacco and second-hand smoke		• Fever	
	Use insect repellant as appropriate.		• Rash	
	Safeguard *all* poisonous agents.		• Nausea	
	Limit intake of alcohol.		• Vomiting	
	Limit intake of caffeine.		• Diarrhea	
	Get sufficient calcium intake.		Modify physical activity to get adequate rest.	
	Practice safe sex.		Get adequate fluids.	
	Get immunizations appropriate for occupation, age, and medical risk.		Modify food intake as appropriate.	
	Get dental exams.		Seek medical care if:	
	Take precautions in hot and cold environments..		• Not better within reasonable time period	
			• Additional symptoms occur	
			• Symptom becomes worse	

Appendix D

Prevention of Injury

"An ounce of prevention is worth a pound of cure"

Injury is physical damage or harm to a person (Webster). Injury prevention is directed toward measures to inhibit the occurrence of an injury to the body. Health care consumers must be aware of their environment and the potential of harm to themselves or others, regardless of age group. Use of tools, equipment, vehicles, weapons, and other items carries the responsibility for safe handling and operation.

| PRIMARY | | SECONDARY | | TERTIARY |
| *Minimize risk for occurrence of injury* | | *Reduce risk of injury becoming worse* | | *Manage risk of complications* |
Health Promotion & Education	Health Protection	Early Diagnosis	Prompt & Adequate Treatment	Rehabilitation & Disability Limitation
Know risk of falls and burns in home environment.	Maintain physical fitness for strength, endurance. and balance--know your limits for exertion.	Immediately administer first aid when injury occurs. After injury, note: • Any loss of mobility or dexterity • Presence of blood • Change in mental status	**EMERGENCIES** *Get immediate medical care for:* • Major trauma • Any eye injury • Any human or animal bite that breaks the skin • Bleeding that can not be stopped After administering first aid, do appropriate self-care for: • Cuts • Burns • Insect bites • Scrapes • Strains • Sprains Seek medical care for any sign of infections.	Keep wounds clean and dry for at least 24 hours. Change dressing daily at a minimum or when soiled. To minimize swelling, rest, elevate, and ice affected area. Progress activity of affected area according to health care provider's instructions. Watch for signs of infection--redness, local swelling, or warmth of affected area. Also any sign of fever.
Be knowledgeable of safe lifting techniques.	Take corrective action or use aids for any visual impairment.			
Be aware of potential or actual domestic violence.	Conduct home safety checks and correct any unsafe findings immediately.			
Be knowledgeable of contact irritants.	Lock-up firearms.			
Be knowledgeable of first aid measures.	Follow manufacturer's instructions for use of products.			
Know hazards of ultraviolet light.	Use sun screen as appropriate.			
Know what to do in hot and cold environments.	Wear appropriate footwear.			
	Wear helmets for horseback, motorcycle, bicycle, scooter riding and skateboarding.			
	Use appropriate protective attire for sporting activities.			

| PRIMARY | | SECONDARY | | TERTIARY |
Minimize risk for occurrence of injury		Reduce risk of injury becoming worse		Manage risk of complications
Health Promotion & Education	Health Protection	Early Diagnosis	Prompt & Adequate Treatment	Rehabilitation & Disability Limitation
	Use gloves, goggles, and hearing protection as personal protective equipment as appropriate to prevent injury to hands, eyes, and ears.			
	Conduct chemical inventory--appropriate labeling, handling and storage precautions.			
	Avoid downed electrical wires.			
	Drive defensively and within speed limit.			
	Wear seat belt at all times.			

Appendix E

Optimal Mental Health

"An ounce of prevention is worth a pound of cure"

Mental well-being is a complex health issue. There are many factors that affect the level of well-being at any given moment. Health care consumers can optimize this level by recognizing their existing behavior patterns, having support systems available, seeking effective communication with others, and working with others to deal with problem areas. Preventive care is focused on awareness of potential problems and effectively communicating feelings to others.

| PRIMARY | | SECONDARY | | TERTIARY |
| Minimize risk for occurrence of problem | | Reduce risk of problem progressing | | Manage risk of complications |
Health Promotion & Education	Health Protection	Early Diagnosis	Prompt & Adequate Treatment	Rehabilitation & Disability Limitation
Be aware of your stress triggers.	Recognize signs and symptoms of anxiety.	Seek medical care if any of the following interfere with work or usual daily activities for more than a brief period:	**EMERGENCIES**	Follow medical plan of care --be active participant in its development.
Explore what anxiety means and what to do.	Practice stress management—		*Get immediate medical care for:*	
Identify your usual coping patterns and be knowledgeable of alternative actions.	• Recognize high stress periods.	• Persistent feeling of sadness, anxiety, or hopelessness	Feeling that you might hurt yourself or others	Assure supply of medication prescribed is adequate at all times to keep diagnosed mood disorders and behavior disorders in check.
	• Increase physical activity and/or use support of others.	• Loss of interest in or no longer enjoy those things formerly	If symptoms interfere with work or usual daily activities, seek medical or mental health assistance as soon as possible.	
Seek information on how to handle loss and deal with grieving.	• Use relaxation techniques.	enjoyed—socializing, hobbies, sex		Seek counseling for anger management.
Be knowledgeable on how to handle the "blues."	Avoid recreational drug use.	• Unexpected change in eating patterns that cause weight gain or loss	For high stress levels:	
Be knowledgeable of assertive behavior and how it differs from passive and aggressive behavior.	Minimize alcohol intake.	• Restlessness or irritability	• Engage in moderate intensity physical activity--take a walk, ride a bicycle, run the vacuum cleaner, etc.	
	Do moderate intensity physical activity for at least 30 minutes daily.	• Insomnia or excessive sleep		
	Schedule "time outs" or breaks.	• Low energy or fatigue	• Talk to someone--family, friend, clergy, counselor.	
Know how to handle aggressive behavior in others.	Eat a variety of food, 3x a day.	• Feeling of worthlessness or guilt		
	Practice being assertive and express your feelings honestly.	• Inability to concentrate, remember, or make decisions		
	Reach out to others, ask about them.			
Seek time management skills.	Develop a support system and use as needed.	Ask others to watch for alteration in behavior or moods.		
	Engage in fun-related activity.			
Be aware of your own needs rather than those inspired by others	Seek humor and the opportunity to laugh.			
—NORMAN COUSINS				

Appendix F

Adult Wellness Checklist

Name: Date of Birth:

Parameters	Goals	Optimal	Date Age	Date Age	Date Age	Date Age	Date Age
Health Risks	Complete Health Risk Assessment.	Annual update					
Health Screening	Maintain health screening schedule for gender and age congruent with U.S. Preventive Task Force recommendations.	Annual Wellness Check					
Weight Control	Maintain weight within recommended parameter.	BMI <25					
	Keep healthy waist circumference.	[M] < 40" [F] <35"					
Healthy Food Choices	Eat breakfast.	Eat daily					
	Avoid fried foods.	< 2 serving/day					
	Limit salt intake.	2400 mg daily (1 tsp)					
	Eat vegetables/fruit.	5 servings/day					
Physical Activity	Do moderate intensity activity.	30 minutes daily					
Sleep/Rest	Feel rested upon awakening.	Practice sleep hygiene.					

Parameters	Goals	Optimal	Date Age	Date Age	Date Age	Date Age	Date Age
Stress Management	Minimize stress level.	Recognize personal stress triggers.					
		Implement effective coping skills.					
Environmental Sensitivity	Minimize injury if involved in accident.	Wear seat belt 100%.					
	Prevent injury while riding bicycle or skating.	Wear helmet 100%.					
	Prevent falls.	Conduct on-going Home Survey.					
	Prevent exposure to chemicals.	Store and handle as directed.					
	Prevent injury from power equipment.	Wear appropriate personal protective equipment.					
	Protect eyes and skin from ultraviolet rays.	Wear sunglasses and apply SPF 30 on skin when exposed to sunlight.					
Substance Use	Use caffeinated beverage in moderation.	Limit to 200-300 mg/day					
	Limit alcoholic beverages.	Males – 2 drinks/day Females – 1 drink/day					
	Avoid tobacco.	None					
	Avoid recreational drug use.	None					
Safe Sex	Avoid unwanted pregnancy.	100% protection					
	Avoid sexually transmitted diseases.	100% protection					
Relationships	Have adequate support systems.	Know who to contact for emotional or financial issues.					
Communication	Use effective communication with others.	Feel comfortable in expressing oneself.					
		Express oneself in assertive manner.					

Parameters	Goals	Optimal	Date Age	Date Age	Date Age	Date Age	Date Age
Infectious Disease Control	Maintain immunizations according to ACIP recommendations.	Update immunizations annually.					
	Prevent transmission of respiratory pathogens to others.	Cover cough or sneeze at all times.					
Health System Utilization	Maintain current record of medical conditions and medications.	Have a copy of personal health profile.					
	Prepare for alternative to provide authorization for medical care when not capable personally.	Have medical directives filed in selected location for others to access.					
	Use effective utilization of health care system = right place, right time, right venue.	Feel confident navigating health care system					
		Seek nursing consultation when uncertain when to seek medical assistance.					
		Have appropriate contact information available.					
Self-Management Skills	Provide self-care for early intervention of health issues.	Seek nursing consultation for health problem.					
		Feel confident to provide self-care for minor injuries or illnesses.					
		Feel confident to handle aggressive behavior in others.					

Appendix G

Requirements Brief for Medicare Annual Wellness Visits

For dates of service on or after January 1, 2011, the Affordable Care Act allows for coverage of the Annual Wellness Visit (AWV), providing Personalized Prevention Plan Services (PPPS).

First Visit *Code G0438*	Subsequent Visit *Code G0439*
Establishment of the individual's medical and family history, which entails, at a minimum, the collection and documentation of: past medical and surgical history, including experiences with illnesses, hospital stays, operations, allergies, injuries, and treatments; use or exposure to medications and supplements, including calcium and vitamins; and medical events in the beneficiary's parents and any siblings and children, including diseases that may be hereditary or place the individual at increased risk.	An update of the individual's medical and family history as defined for the first Annual Wellness Visit.
Establishment of a list of current providers and suppliers that are regularly involved in providing medical care to the individual	An update of the list of current providers and suppliers that are regularly involved in providing medical care to the individual, as that list was developed for the first annual wellness visit providing Personalized Prevention Plan Services

First Visit Code G0438	Subsequent Visit Code G0439
Measurement of the individual's height, weight, body mass index (or waist circumference, if appropriate), blood pressure, and other routine measurements as deemed appropriate, based on the individual's medical and family history	Measurement of an individual's weight (or waist circumference), blood pressure, and other routine measurements as deemed appropriate, based on the individual's medical and family history*
Detection of any cognitive impairment, defined as an assessment of an individual's cognitive function by direct observation, with due consideration of information obtained by of way of patient report, concerns raised by family members, friends, caretakers, or other	Detection of any cognitive impairment, defined as an assessment of an individual's cognitive function by direct observation, with due consideration of information obtained by way of patient report, concerns raised by family members, friends, caretakers, or other
Review of the individual's potential (risk factors) for depression, including current or past experiences with depression or other mood disorders, based on the use of an appropriate screening instrument for persons without a current diagnosis of depression, which the health professional as defined in this section may select from various available screening questions or standardized questionnaires designed for this purpose and recognized by national professional medical organizations *Unique to the first visit*	N/A
Review of the individual's functional ability and level of safety, based on direct observation or the use of appropriate screening questions or a screening questionnaire, which the health professional as defined in this section may select from various available screening questions or standardized questionnaires designed for this purpose and recognized by national professional medical organizations. Review must include, at a minimum, an assessment of: hearing impairment; ability to successfully perform activities of daily living; fall risk; and home safety. *Unique to the first visit*	N/A
Establish a written screening schedule, such as a checklist, for the next 5 to 10 years as appropriate, based on recommendations of the USPSTF and the ACIP, and the individual's health status, screening history, and age appropriate preventive services covered by Medicare.	Update to the written screening schedule for the individual that was developed at the first Annual Wellness Visit.

First Visit Code G0438	Subsequent Visit Code G0439
Establish a list of risk factors and conditions for which primary, secondary or tertiary interventions are recommended or are underway, including any mental health conditions or any such risk factors or conditions that have been identified through an initial preventive physical examination and a list of treatment options and their associated risks and benefits.	Update the list of risk factors and conditions for which primary, secondary or tertiary interventions are recommended or are underway for the individual that was developed at the first Annual Wellness Visit.
Furnish personalized health advice and a referral, as appropriate, to health education or preventive counseling services or programs aimed at reducing identified risk factors and improving self management, or community-based lifestyle interventions to reduce health risks and promote self-management and wellness, including weight loss, physical activity, smoking cessation, fall prevention, and nutrition.	Furnish personalized health advice and a referral, as appropriate, to health education or preventive counseling services or programs aimed at reducing identified risk factors and improving self management, or community-based lifestyle interventions to reduce health risks and promote self-management and wellness, including weight loss, physical activity, smoking cessation, fall prevention, and nutrition.

Source: Centers for Medicare and Medicaid Services (CMS). "*Annual Wellness Visit Benefit Overview.*" (2011), http://www.cms.gov/Outreach-and-Education/ Medicare-Learning-Network-MLN/MLNProducts/downloads/ mps_guide_web-061305.pdf

Appendix H

Safeguarding Your Home

Safeguarding Your Home

According to the National Safety Council, accidents are the leading cause of death for children and young to middle-aged adults in the United States . It is imperative that you take measures to minimize the risk of an accident in your home, an area in which you can have a great amount of control. Check these areas routinely:

All Areas

1. All pathways are free of clutter.
2. Loose throw rugs are tacked down, held in place with carpet tape or non-slip pad, or removed.
3. All chemicals (cleaning agents, rodent poisons, weed/insect killers, fertilizers) are tightly capped or closed and properly stored out of reach of children.
4. Hot water thermostat is set between 120 and 125°F.
5. Extension cords do not run under rugs or across pathways.
6. There is limited use of extension cords to avoid over-loading.
7. Flammable or heating items are kept away from curtains or draperies.

8. Smoke detector is placed in every room or space enclosed by walls and checked monthly.

9. Nonskid floor wax is used.

10. Any loose floor board or loose/frayed carpet is repaired immediately.

11. Candles are in stable holders and fully extinguished after use, before bedtime, or before leaving home.

12. Repair loose furniture legs or arms immediately.

13. Flashlights are available for power outrages.

Kitchen

1. Liquor is properly stored out of reach of children.

2. Knives, scissors, ice picks, and other sharp instruments are stored separately in a safe place out of reach of children.

3. Frayed cords on electrical appliances are fixed or replaced.

4. Towels, curtains, and other flammable materials hang a safe distance from the stove.

5. Multipurpose (ABC) fire extinguisher is available and checked monthly.

6. Exhaust vent over the kitchen range is clean and free of grease build-up.

7. Pot holders are within easy reach.

8. Infrequently used appliances are left unplugged.

9. All appliances have a 3-prong plug.

10. A ground fault circuit interrupt (GFCI) outlet is installed in any outlet near the sink.

11. A sturdy step stool is available to reach high cabinets.

Bathroom

1. Glass containers are removed or replaced with plastic containers.

2. Electrical appliances (hair dryer, hair curling iron, electric shaver) are unplugged and properly stored.

3. Outdated medications in medicine cabinet are discarded.

4. Tub and/or shower have a nonskid surface, adhesive grippers placed on the floor or nonslip mat and a railing along the wall to help prevent falls.

5. A ground fault circuit interrupt (GFCI) outlet is installed in any outlet near the sink.

Living Room/Family Room

1. Bookcases, TV stands, or other tall furniture cannot tip over or are secured to the wall.
2. Low coffee tables, magazine racks, footrests, or plants are not in the pathway.
3. Light switches are available at entrances to the room.
4. Fireplace screen fits snuggly and fire is extinguished at bedtime.

Bedroom(s)

1. Heavy furniture, especially chests of drawers, cannot tip over or are secured to the wall.
2. Electric blankets are left unplugged and are not tucked in.
3. Gas and electric heating devices are turned off at night (sleeping hours).
4. Night illumination is available in bedroom/hallway.
5. Drawers are closed when not in use.
6. Bedside lamp or switch is within easy reach.

Laundry Area

1. Clothes dryer is properly vented.
2. Dryer vent is free of lint and other debris.

Stairways and Steps

1. Light switches are at both the top and bottom of the stairs.
2. There is enough lighting to see each step and the top and bottom landings.
3. Handrails are available.
4. No objects are left on the stairs--shoes, books, toys, tools, or other clutter.
5. Bare wood steps are covered by non-slip treads.
6. Frayed or loose carpeting or boards are repaired immediately.

Garage or Basement

1. Freezers are locked or secured.
2. Infrequently used refrigerators, storage lockers, or other places are secured.
3. Strong, rigid ladders are used and kept in good repair.
4. Walls and beams are free of protruding nails.

5. Gasoline and other flammable materials are stored in airtight containers away from any heat source (outside the home if possible).

6. Multipurpose (ABC) fire extinguisher is available and checked monthly.

7. Wastepaper is kept away from the furnace and neatly stacked.

8. Fuses or circuit breakers are the right size.

9. Continual problem with blown fuses or tripped breaker is checked for overload or short circuit.

Attic or Storage Area

1. Items are stored away from heat ducts, chimneys, or exposed wiring and such in a manner that they will not topple over.

2. Damaged wiring or insulation is repaired immediately.

Around the House

1. Entrances are well lit.

2. Outdoor porches/decks, landings, and walkways are kept clear of ice in the winter weather.

3. Walkways are kept clear of tripping hazards.

4. Yard is free from holes, stones, broken glass, nail-studded boards, garden tools, and other litter.

Additional tips are available to childproof homes

Appendix I

Situational Leadership Actions to Influence Behavior

Leadership Style	Health Care Consumer		Professional Nurse Actions	Goal
	Readiness Level	Characteristics		
S1 Directing	Unable; unwilling	Has little experience or information. Lacks specific skills. Has low confidence.	Individual needs to be told what to do, when, where, how and who is to do it. May need to provide a specific check list, a sequence of actions, list of responsibilities, and frequently monitor progress.	*Develop Growth*
S2 Coaching	Unable; willing	Does not have necessary knowledge or skill but are eager to learn. Is making an effort, may have some relevant skill or knowledge. Task or behavior may be new to individual. Needs direction and supervision.	Individual needs guidance and direction for accomplishing the task. Health care personnel need to be supportive of individual's efforts to build self-esteem. Involve individual in decision-making to promote or restore commitment. Several options can be suggested for doing things and encourage the individual to try them out and select what works best.	

Leadership Style	Health Care Consumer		Professional Nurse Actions	Goal
	Readiness Level	Characteristics		
S3 Supporting	Able, unwilling	Experienced and capable but lacks confidence to go it alone or motivation to do it quickly or well. Has already demonstrated they know how to perform or complete the task. May be apprehensive about doing task or changing behavior	Individual needs support and encouragement in order to build confidence as well as an opportunity for dialogue and discussion to work through problems. Individual does not need a great deal of structure or direction.	
S4 Empowering	Able; willing	Experienced, competent, and comfortable with own ability to do task well or manage behavior.	Individual needs very little guidance and direction and does not need a lot of support. Touch base periodically to make sure individual stays on track and provide feedback to let know efforts are noticed.	

Appendix J

Chronic Disease Electronic Management System Overview

The Chronic Disease Management System (CDEMS) is a software application developed by the Washington State Diabetes Prevention Program in 2002. It is a Microsoft Access database application designed to assist medical providers and disease managers in tracking the care of patients with chronic health conditions. CDEMS is pre-coded to track diabetes, asthma and adult health but is customizable to change those tracking measures or define measures for monitoring other chronic health conditions.

The tracking measures for any health condition can be defined in CDEMS. This includes related diagnosis, needs, meds, services and labs. Measures are created and customized in the user-friendly CDEMS SetUp Wizard. A customized tickler system can be set-up to remind providers of labs and services due dates and alert when test values are out of the target range. Service result pick lists and lab validation rules can be customized to ensure clean and consistent collection of data. The "Create-A-Report" and "Create–A-List" templates in the reports program allow development of customized summary reports and intervention lists based on each clinic's unique setup parameters.

Many Electronic Medical Records (EMRs) are working on a way to manipulate data for population management/analysis. If there's a way to export data from your EMR, CDEMS can conceivably work with available data in a variety of formats: HL7, comma delimited, Excel, Access, txt files. Many organizations have developed data-sharing interfaces between their EMR and CDEMS, but an easy-to-use, stand-ardized interface is not available. The number of EMR vendors and variable configuration issues are significant obstacles to building a one-size-fits-all interface. Still, the ability to export data is an important feature to consider in choosing an EMR. Data exchange with other systems can enable the use of CDEMS population-based reporting tools. Automating that exchange of information requires technical expertise to build a custom interface with cooperation from the system vendor to obtain data and map data elements. Many clinics continue to use CDEMS for tracking chronic conditions until the EMR is fully implemented and reporting capability tested. Others are resigned to continuing with dual systems until better, more affordable information technology solutions are available.

CDEMS is flexible and easily modified to meet specific needs of an independent provider, a clinic system, provider group, community health center, or quality improvement initiative. With easy-to-use report-building templates, data can be transformed by a non-technical user to useful information about care provided or identification of patients falling through the cracks. CDEMS is often the first step in transitioning to electronic record management, requiring little capital investment and a low level of technical expertise to get started. A lab interface is available for electronically downloading lab results from several major labs.

Source: *CDEMS Basics*, Chronic Disease Electronic Management System (CDEMS) User Network. Additional information available at CDEMS website under the headings:
   ◆ Introduction to CDEMS ◆ CDEMS Data Entry ◆ CDEMS Report.

Appendix K

Look-up Table Example for Summary Health Care Record

S01 SKIN

Medical Conditions/Risks	
692.9	Dermatitis, Contact NOS
690.1	Dermatitis, Seborrhea
696.1	Psoriasis
054.9	Herpes Simplex
053.0	Herpes Zoster
682.9	Cellulitis
707.0	Decubitus Ulcer
110.0	Tinea Capitis
110.4	Tinea Pedis
110.1	Tinea Ungulum
133.0	Scabies
706.1	Acne
692.71	Sunburn
940-949	Burns
M8090/3	Basal Cell Carcinoma
M8070/3	Squamous Cell Carcinoma
M8720/3	Malignant Melanoma
870-897	Open wound
707.9	Ulceration

Medical Conditions/Risks

708.9	Urticaria, unspecific
V15.9	Health Risk--Skin Cancer (Prolonged exposure to sun)
V15.9	Health Risk--Contact dermatitis (Exposure to chemical agents)
V15.9	Health Risk--Burns (Exposure to steam/hot water)
V15.9	Health Risk--Injury (Works with power equipment)
V16.8	+ Family History --Skin Cancer

Services/ Interventions

I01-Hospitalization	
I02-ER Visit	
I03-Surgery	Skin Excision
I04-Provider Encounter	
I05-Special Procedure	Skin Biopsy
I05-Special Procedure	Laceration Repair
I05-Special Procedure	I & D
I05-Special Procedure	Wound Care
I06-Specific Exam	Skin Survey
I06-Specific Exam	Visual Foot Exam
I07-Specific Test	
I08-Lab Test	
I09-Diagnostic Imaging	
I10-Pharmaceutical	
I11-Consult/Advise	
I11-Consult/Advise	Use appropriate Personal Protective Equipment (PPE)
I12-Counsel/Coach	Skin Protection
I12-Counsel/Coach	Periodic Skin Survey for Changes in Skin Lesions
I13-Referral	Dermatology

Pharmaceutical Agents

▶ ALLERGIC REACTION

● Adverse Reaction

Topical Antifungal	Terbinafine HCL *Lamisil*®
Topical Antifungal	Clotrimazole *Lotrimin*®, *Mycelex*®
Topical Antiviral	Acyclovir *Zovirax*®

Pharmaceutical Agents	
Topical Antiviral	Docosanol *Abreva®*
Topical Antibiotic	Bacitracin *Baciguent®*
Topical Antibiotic	Erythromycin
Topical Antibiotic	Tetracycline HCL *Achromycin®*
Pediculicide	Permethrin *Nix®*
Scabicide	Lindane *Kwell®*
Topical Corticosteroid	Hydrocortizone *Cortizone®*
Topical Corticosteroid	Hydrocortizone acetate *Cortaid®*
Topical Corticosteroid	Triamcinolone acetonide *Aristocort®*, *Kenalog®*
Topical Antipruritic	Doxepin *Zonalon®*

Appendix L

Entry Categories for Summary Health Care Record

Medical Conditions/Health Risks

- System (S00-S12)
- Code
- Name
- Comments [Self Reported], [Documented on Medical Records], [Managed by Secondary or Tertiary Provider], [Flow Sheet Available], [Occupational Risk Factor], etc.
- Current/Past (C/P)

NOTE: Family member(s) with condition can be noted under comments for + Family History –Paternal/Maternal Grandparents, Parents, Siblings

Services/Interventions

- System (S00-S12)
- Category
  - I01 Hospitalization
  - I02 ER Visit
  - I03 Surgery
  - I04 Provider Encounter
  - I05 Special Procedure [Laser], [Sigmoidoscope], etc.

- - I06 Specific Exam Parameter [B/P], [BMI], [Head Circumference], [Foot Exam], etc.
  - I07 Specific Test [Doppler], [Audiogram], [Cognitive Impairment], etc.
  - I08 Lab Test
  - I09 Diagnostic Imaging
  - I10 Pharmaceutical [Immunization], [Corticosteroid], etc.
  - I11 Consult/Advise
  - I12 Counsel/Coach
  - I13 Referral
- Name
- Date
- Comments/Findings
- Location
- Current/Past (C/P)

NOTE: Category items are given identification code to maintain order of categories on a report.

Pharmaceutical Agents

- System (S00-S12)
- Type
- Name
- Date
- Action [START], [▲▲(change increase)], [▲▼(change decrease)], [STOP]
- Dose and Frequency
- Current/Past (C/P)

NOTE: Under related category note: [▶ Allergic Reaction] or [● Adverse Reaction] followed by name of pharmaceutical agent in the next column. Medication Management by Secondary or Tertiary Provider can be noted by use of grayscale.

Appendix M

Medical Plan of Care

Name:	**DOB:**
Medical Condition:	**ICD-9 Code:**

Specific Goal(s):

Prescribed Medications/Pharmaceutical Agents

Home Self-Management Activities Outlined:

Daily Medical Monitoring: [ ] None

Treatment(s): [ ] None

Dietary Limitations: [ ] None

Activity Limitations: [ ] None

Medical Testing/Evaluation/Referral Requested:

Requested F/U Interval:
[ ] Every 4 months [ ] Every 6 Months [ ] Annually [ ] Other _____

COMMENTS

Medical Provider	**Contact Information**
	Location:
_____	
Signature	Telephone Number:
	Email:
_____	FAX:
Printed Name Title	

Appendix N

Matching Workload to Available Professional Nurse Time

Forecasting workload and matching resources is a management challenge. There is no guarantee what was forecasted will occur. Management expertise is required to monitor and adjust a changing workload to resource availability. Some calculations can be made based on hours available for care and an estimate of hours required for anticipated workload. Forecasting workload for a year is to justify staff positions. In ambulatory care, projecting workload on a weekly basis is linked to a time schedule and type of appointments for health care providers.

Calculating productive time available

Productive time is required to accomplish workload and is generally calculated:

$$\frac{\text{Productive Time}}{2080} = \% \text{ Productive Time}$$

or state minimum allowance and multiply 2080 times 2080
(i.e., .80 x 2080 = 1664 hrs)

$$\frac{\text{Non-Productive Time}}{2080} = \% \text{ Non-Productive}$$

or state maximum allowance and multiply 2080 Time times 2080
(i.e., .20 x 2080 = 416 hrs)

Equation Components

1. *Full Time Equivalent* – the universal number other calculations are relative to 40 hours per week times 52 weeks = 2080 hours per year

2. *Productive Hours* – paid time engaged in work activities related to direct services to health care consumer. This represents billable time for providers. For all clinical staff, this incorporates direct and indirect care activities.

3. *Non-Productive Time* – paid time NOT engaged in direct services to health care consumer.

- Paid Time Off ("Banked Hours")
    - Vacation
    - Sick
    - Holiday
- Breaks
- Mandatory Training/Education
- Meetings
- Administrative--peer/employee performance evaluations, support requestIndependent Study--research data collection and analysis, literature review
- Conference/consultation--not specific consumer related

Workload is projected by forecasting the number and type of services. An example follows that converts projected workload into estimated time requirements for professional nurses.

Estimated Time Requirement for Professional Nurses – An Example

Panel Size: 1200
Productivity Rate: 80% (Non-productive time for one FTE cannot exceed 416 hours or 52 days/year)

1. *Forecast Volume* (projected number per service)

	Month	Year
New Check-in Visits	3	36
Annual Check-in Visits	100	1200
Consulting/counseling 10 min/enrollee		2 hour/enrollee

2. Calculate Units of Service for Workload Activities (time element allotted per service)

	RN	NP
New Check-in Visits	18	1.5
Annual Check-in Visits	12	1.0
Consulting/counseling	12/enrollee	----

3. Forecast Workload by Units of Service

Projected Workload for a Year

New Check-in Visits	RN	648	NP	54	(23.4 hr)*
Annual Check-in Visits	RN	14,400	NP	1200	(520 hr)*
Consulting/counselling	RN	14,400			
TOTAL		29,448		1254	(543.4 hr)

4. Transform to Staffing Requirements

1 FTE = 2080 hours @ 80% Productivity Rate = 1664 productive + 416 non-productive hours

RN: 29,448 units of service x 10 minutes = 294,480 minutes divided by 60 = 4908 hours divided by 1664 = 2.95 FTE

Paid time = 6135 hours (4908 productive hours + 1228 non-productive hours)

NP: 1254 units of services x 10 minutes = 12,540 minutes divided by 60 = 209 hours + 543.4 hours = 752.4 hours. divided by 1664 = .45 FTE

Paid Time = 936 hours (745 productive hours + 191 non-productive hours)

NOTE: Assumes on-going consulting or counseling is responsibility of RN. This does not preclude NP providing the service and accounting as NP unit of service.

* Exam time in hours. NP will be using CPT codes for comprehensive preventive medicine exam. Allotted 20 minutes per exam plus 10 minutes per exam for Well Woman and adolescent with projection of 60% of the population.

www.ingramcontent.com/pod-product-compliance
Lightning Source LLC
Chambersburg PA
CBHW070402200326
41518CB00011B/2032